SOVIET SCIENTISTS AND THE STATE

In recent years there has been much discussion of the negative social and economic consequences thought to arise from the continuing highly centralised character of Communist Party rule in the Soviet Union. Few areas of academic interest place these issues in sharper relief than the study of the political relations of Soviet natural scientists.

In so far as the division of labour in the natural sciences transcends national and ideological boundaries, Soviet scientists are susceptible to a variety of professional influences which crosscut official institutional hierarchies through which Communist Party supervision is exercised. As science is generally considered to thrive on unimpeded personal communication, some of the conditions regarded as essential for effective research conflict with the established forms of political control prevailing in the Soviet Union.

The working environment of Soviet natural scientists thus provides a fruitful context in which to assess the consequences of the measures adopted by the party to maintain its dominance and also an appropriate base from which to explore some important sources of change in contemporary Soviet politics.

Dr Peter Kneen is Lecturer in Politics at the University of Durham. He was previously Research Fellow in the Centre for Russian and East European Studies at the University of Birmingham.

SOVIET SCIENTISTS AND THE STATE

An Examination of the Social and Political Aspects of Science in the USSR

Peter Kneen

State University of New York Press
Albany

First published in U.S.A. by
State University of New York Press, Albany

For information, address State University of New York Press,
State University Plaza, Albany, N.Y., 12246

Printed in Hong Kong

Library of Congress Cataloging in Publication Data

Kneen, Peter.
Soviet scientists and the state.

Bibliography: p.
Includes index.
1. Scientists—Soviet Union. 2. Science—Social
aspects—Soviet Union. 3. Communism and science.
I. Title.
Q149.S65K59   1985   306′.45′0947   83–26931

ISBN 0–87395–896–9

Contents

Contents

List of Tables

Acknowledgements

In the course of writing this book I have incurred numerous intellectual debts, many of which are owed to current and former members of the Centre for Russian and East European Studies at the University of Birmingham, with which I was associated both as a post-graduate student and as a member of staff. In particular, I would like to thank Professor R. W. Davies for his generous advice and encouragement over many years. I am similarly indebted to Dr Ron Amann and Professor Moshe Lewin, the latter now at the University of Pennsylvania, who supervised a doctoral thesis in which many of the ideas which have now found expression in this book originally took shape. My thanks are also due to Dr Mary McAuley of Essex University, to Dr Julian Cooper of the Centre and to Dr R. A. Lewis, formerly at the Centre but now at Exeter University, all of whom have greatly helped me to clarify my ideas about the subject of this book. Dr Stephen Fortescue of the Australian National University sent me valuable comments on the manuscript which I gratefully acknowledge.

I would also like to take the opportunity to express my appreciation for the invaluable service of the Alexander Baykov Library at the Centre and, in particular, to thank Ms Jenny Brine, the librarian, and Mr Hugh Jenkins, the information officer, for their selfless efforts on my behalf. In the course of researching this field I have also called on the Inter-Library Loans Service many times and would like to register my thanks to the Inter-Library Loans Department of Durham University Library and also to the staff of the British Library Lending Division at Boston Spa without whose efficient support life would have been much harder.

My thanks are due to the British Council, through whose good offices I have visited the Soviet Union on a number of occasions, most recently in the winter of 1980–1, and to the Soviet scholars whom I have been fortunate enough to meet over the years. I am also indebted to the University of Durham for granting me sabbatical leave in the Michaelmas Term of 1981 and for paying for me to visit the Centre for Russian and East European Studies during the Easter vacation of 1982 in order to complete my research. I am also glad to have the chance to thank Mrs Dorothy Anson and Mrs Jean Richardson for their patient secretarial help in preparing the manuscript of this book.

Finally, in writing this book I have drawn on material originally published in the *British Journal of Political Science*. I would like to thank Cambridge University Press for granting me permission to do this.

PETER KNEEN

1 Introduction: The Social and Political Relations of Soviet Natural Scientists

THE ORGANISATION OF THE BOOK

This book contains three interrelated themes. The first concerns Soviet natural scientists as members of a social group. The second considers the relationship between this group and the institutions in which scientists are employed and carry out their work. The third deals with the political context of science and, in particular, the influence of the Communist Party on scientists and vice versa.

The purpose of Chapters 2 and 3 is to build up a social profile of natural scientists as a social group. As a necessary preliminary step the second chapter opens with a discussion of the definition of a 'scientific worker' as used in Soviet statistical compilations and then describes some of the features of the Soviet fundamental research system of which the USSR Academy of Sciences is the main component. Following this, the question of the elite status of natural scientists is considered in relation to academic, economic and political criteria. In Chapter 3 the educational background and demographic character-istics of Soviet natural scientists are analysed and the broader social and political implications of these features are discussed.

Chapter 4 moves away from the description of the objective socio-economic status and political position of natural scientists and considers them as the members of real groups which form around the research problems on which they are engaged. It is in this kind of group that problems are defined, results evaluated and professional recognition distributed. The direction and significance of scientific work, as well as the professional standing of scientists, are influenced by such groups, networks, or scientific communities, as they are some-times called. The cognitive and social aspects of science can thus be seen to be intimately linked.

Because science is universal, the division of labour does not neatly fit into national or institutional boundaries. The formal hierarchies and administrative subdivisions of a nation's scientific institutions do not, therefore, fully correspond with the professional relations which grow up among the scientists employed in them. Although often in receipt of state funds, neither the problems on which scientists work, nor the results which they receive are entirely defined or assessed by their administrative superiors. In so far as recognition is allocated through informal scientific communities, scientists have a source of independent criteria by which to judge the scientific standing of their superiors and the professional authoritativeness of the hierarchies which they surmount.

In Chapter 5, the relationship between the informal structure of scientific communities and the formal institutional arrangements of the establishments in which their participants are employed is discussed. Particular attention is paid to the character of leadership in research establishments and the way in which such a decentralised activity as science is accommodated by the centralised system of state planning operating through the USSR Academy of Sciences and its kindred institutions.

Academic establishments are not the only components in the institutional framework within which scientific research and academic teaching takes place in the Soviet Union. An important role is also played by the Soviet Communist Party. This role is described and its significance discussed in Chapters 6 and 7. The Communist Party's responsibilities are not confined to political functions such as generating and disseminating propaganda: it also plays a key role in the supervision of scientists and the research they undertake. These aspects of the party's work are closely associated in the way in which it interprets its activities in science. Essentially the party asserts that effective research is dependent upon the success with which the party's supervisory and ideological roles are carried out in scientific institutions. An examination of the validity of this claim forms an important part of the two chapters concerned with the political context of science in the USSR.

SOVIET SCIENTISTS AND THE STATE: SOME RECURRING QUESTIONS

In order to understand the relationship between the Soviet state and natural scientists it is necessary to distinguish between the party and the ministerial hierarchies in terms of both structure and function. In terms of their functions, the ministerial hierarchies, which are ultimately subordinated to the USSR Council of Ministers, are each responsible for administering a branch of the Soviet economy. In this sense their organisational arrangements reflect their single area of responsibility. Here, it may be pointed out, the USSR Academy of Sciences enjoys a status and carries responsibilities analogous to those of a ministry in the area of fundamental research in the natural and social sciences.

The party's structure also reflects its functions but, unlike the narrower ministries which are concerned only with their respective branches, the party is comprehensively involved in all aspects of Soviet life. As mentioned earlier, the party not only concerns itself with ideology but also with the supervision of policy-making and with all stages of its execution. This ubiquity is reflected in the party's organisational structure. Whereas the ministerial hierarchies radiate outwards from Moscow, each one forming a spoke in a kind of immense administrative wheel, the party supervises the making of policy through its central organs and checks its execution through the regional, local and primary organisations. Only at the lowest level is the party organised in terms of the 'branch' principle, in that its primary organisations, which number upwards of 400 000, are predominantly located in the place of work.[1]

The implications of the differences in the organisational arrangements between the ministries, or in this case the USSR Academy of Sciences, and the party for understanding the relationship between the natural scientists and the state consist in the following. Because the USSR Academy of Sciences, and indeed the other hierarchies of the Soviet research and development and higher educational systems, are organised in terms of the 'branch' principle, they are very much more intimately exposed to the inner workings of science than are the local, regional and central party organs which supervise them. Scientific institutions might thus be expected to be more responsive to the characteristics of science than the party. This is, in general, the case. Although it should not be exaggerated, scientific hierarchies and plans have, to a degree, absorbed the informality and responded to the autonomy of science.

The party, in comparison, is much less open to these kinds of influences. Only at its primary level, the level at which its rank-and-file members are organised, is the party fully exposed to the numerous working environments over which it exercises administrative and ideological supervision. In this sense the themes in terms of which this book is organised represent significant distinctions in Soviet society as well as convenient categories. This is because the institutions of Soviet science, in particular the USSR Academy of Sciences, lie at a point somewhere between the decentralised informal communities of natural scientists on the one hand, and the centralised Soviet Communist Party on the other.

As implied by these distinctions, the relationship between scientists and the state, considered here to consist of the party and ministerial hierarchies, is not one-way. Undoubtedly its impact on science and scientists remains considerable but there are channels through which reciprocal influences can flow. Whilst most of these are located in the USSR Academy of Sciences, the party is not hermetically sealed off from the society it governs. The supervision of policy-making means that the Central Committee apparatus and the Secretariat are on the receiving end of the considered views of the leading members of the USSR Academy of Sciences in the field of science policy. In its official capacity as the leading and guiding organ in Soviet society the CPSU, through its Central Committee, attaches its authority to a wide variety of policies which emanate from numerous disparate sources reflecting influences which are not confined to the party apparatus.

In so far as those who occupy influential positions in the USSR Academy of Sciences enjoy the recognition of their colleagues, their authority is based, at least in part, on informal scientific communities. These communities transcend the institutional boundaries of the research establishments for which such leading scientists may be responsible and the administrative divisions of the USSR Academy of Sciences in which they may hold high office. They are thus well placed to appreciate the important part played by informal communities in the advancement of science. It is not surprising, therefore, that, in the past, the most committed advocates of strengthening informal contacts in science have been those whose work has received the widest international recognition, thus lending their views an independent source of authority not readily available to those employed in other professions in the Soviet Union.[2]

The upper reaches of the scientific hierarchy are not the only sources of influence on the party apparatus. The primary party organisations located in scientific research organisations and other scholarly establishments such as universities are exposed, through the functions they perform and through their rank-and-file membership, to the ideas and practices which constitute the research environment. However, the party's territorial organisational structure acts as a safeguard against the absorption by the party apparatus of the ethos of science or, indeed, any of the wide spectrum of working environments in which its primary organisations operate. This is because the primary organisations of research establishments are subordinated to many different district party organisations. The potential collective influence of scientists on the party is thus dispersed by its territorial structure at every level above the very lowest one.[3]

THE PARTY'S CONFLICTING GOALS: DOMINANCE *v.* EFFICIENCY

In maintaining its centralised structure and ideological monopoly the party imposes conditions on society which are widely considered, both inside and outside the USSR, to be inimical to the achievement of the nation's potential in the economy and elsewhere.[4] One of the most useful consequences of studying the social and political aspects of science in the USSR is that the tension between centralisation and decentralisation is exhibited with particular clarity in this sphere. In consequence, the image of the party's role in science as expressed in Soviet ideology is also placed in sharp relief by the working experiences of Soviet scientists.

As the division of labour in the natural sciences is international, the informal communities which develop among scientists are not restricted to any particular nation any more than they are to any particular set of institutions. The intellectual problems that preoccupy Soviet scientists, the evaluation of their results and the recognition they receive are thus influenced by communities of scientists which extend beyond the borders of the Soviet Union or the socialist world. This is one of the most important sources of tension, for although the Communist Party leaders have for many years accepted the universal character of the natural sciences, they claim that the differences between socialist and capitalist societies place contrasting social and political responsibilities on the scientists of these respective systems.

According to the Communist Party, Soviet society provides an environment uniquely well suited to the advancement of science and the humane exploitation of its results. In this it allegedly contrasts with the situation existing under capitalism where scientific advance is said to contribute to unemployment and the growth of parasitical occupations.[5] The claimed coalescence of the interests of the scientists and the Soviet state removes any grounds for conflict by presenting party policy as expressing the consensus of scientific opinion in the Soviet Union.

This image of the role of the Soviet state in science can, like any other statement, be illustrated through the use of selective evidence. There can be no doubting the generous level of investment in science. The USSR Academy of Sciences is unique in the degree to which it concentrates the nation's resources on fundamental research. The creation of its institutions, together with those of the republican academies, the industrial research and development network and the immense higher educational system are almost entirely post-revolutionary achievements.

Yet the Soviet scientific system does not function as well as it should.[6] Contributing to the explanation of its disappointing performance is the evidence which shows that the cultural isolation of the Soviet Union, and the consequent insulation of Soviet scientists from their counterparts abroad, reduces the effectiveness of the Soviet effort in fundamental research. Isolation produces a disproportionate loss of information and motivation among Soviet scientists and reduces the impact which scientifically significant problems can make within the Soviet planning system.

In consequence, the social and economic needs of Soviet society, as interpreted by the organs of the state, exert considerable pressure on those composing the plans to be carried out by the USSR Academy of Sciences. The claims of technology, as opposed to science, are lent additional weight by the ideology. In conformity with its materialist assumptions, Marxism-Leninism perceives science as reflecting the changing structure of its economic and social environment. It is on this basis that the concept of pure science is repudiated in the Soviet Union, being replaced by the notion of fundamental research, which is usually taken to mean research concerned with the theoretical and exploratory stages of new technologies rather than with the pursuit of new knowledge for its own sake.

The international division of labour in science makes it more vulnerable than most other activities, including other intellectual pursuits, to measures designed to preserve the cultural isolation of the Soviet population. Whereas the industrial worker may seek political freedoms in order to express grievances concerning conditions of employment, the restrictions on freedoms of association, movement and communication, especially when involving foreigners, deprive scientists of important means of carrying out their work itself. It is in this sense that the ideological image of the role of the state in science can be placed in a starkly negative relief, for the means of sustaining the dominance of the Communist Party, at least in its present form, contradict the aims of its science policy which are concerned to increase the effectiveness of Soviet fundamental research.[7]

This conflict of aims affects the bottom as well as the top of the party hierarchy. The role of the primary party organisations in scientific research establishments is predicated on the assertion that effective science can only be carried out in institutions where the level of ideological commitment is high and the supervisory functions of the party energetically performed. Scientists are, therefore, required to conform to, or at least not obviously challenge, the image of unique compatibility between the state and the scientists propagated by the party. As conformity in this respect may help to open up individual opportunities to maintain more direct and regular contacts with foreign colleagues than might otherwise be possible, participation in informal communities tends to be treated by the party as a method of political control rather than as a way of improving the overall performance of Soviet scientists.

The theme of tension between the internationality of science and the centralised state runs through virtually all aspects of this analysis of the social and political relations of Soviet scientists. In the institutional sense, informal scientific communities present Soviet political leaders with a means of improving the effectiveness of their research effort at the cost of loosening their control over scientists. In the ideological sense, the question may be asked as to whether the opening up of Soviet scientists to the fuller influence of international scientific communities would present a more serious challenge to the credibility of Soviet propaganda than the threat already posed by the conflicting goals of the party towards science and its ambiguous role in relation to scientists.

2 Soviet Natural Scientists: Institutions and Status

NATURAL SCIENTISTS AND THE ACADEMIES OF SCIENCES

The conception of science in the English-speaking world is narrower than the Russian equivalent *nauka*, which more closely corresponds to the English words 'knowledge' or 'scholarship', since it incorporates the social sciences and the humanities as well as the natural and applied sciences.

The occupational category *nauchnyi rabotnik*, or scientific worker, used in the compilations published by the Soviet Central Statistical Administration is, therefore, more diverse than might at first be thought. It includes the following:

Academicians, full members and corresponding members of academies of sciences; all persons with the higher degree of doctor of sciences or candidate of sciences or the academic title of professor, associate professor, senior research worker, junior research worker or assistant, irrespective of the place or character of work; persons carrying out research work in research establishments and research and teaching work in higher educational establishments irrespective of whether they have a higher degree or academic title or not, and also specialists having neither a higher degree nor an academic title but systematically carrying out research work in industrial enterprises, in project, project-design and project-technological organisations according to a thematic plan of research work approved in accordance with established procedures.[1]

Clearly not all of the almost 1 400 000 scientific workers recorded by the Central Statistical Administration at the end of 1980 were scientists in the usual English sense of the term.[2] Upwards of 40 per cent of them might more appropriately be described as technologists.

About another fifth were engaged in the humanities, the social sciences, education and law. A further fifth were scientists in the English sense of mathematicians and physicists, chemists, biologists and geologists. The remaining fifth consisted of those engaged in medical, pharmaceutical, agricultural and veterinary sciences.[3]

However, not all scientific workers, including the natural scientists, are systematically engaged in research. Over a third of all Soviet scientific workers are employed by higher educational institutions of different kinds where opportunities for research vary considerably.[4] Whilst the staff of the leading universities and polytechnical institutions are, in general, able to conduct research systematically, either in their own institutions or in collaboration with nearby research establishments, opportunities for research sharply decline as one moves away from the established centres. Outside the major cities and the research satellites of the Moscow region and Siberia, facilities are frequently inadequate and staff lack the means to carry out serious research over and above often heavy teaching commitments.[5] This affects all disciplines, but can prove to be an insurmountable obstacle in experimental research where sophisticated equipment is usually required.[6]

In order to avoid confusion arising from differences in the English and Russian understanding of 'science', the term scientific worker will always be used to denote the general occupational category *nauchnyi rabotnik* as defined in official Soviet statistics compiled by the Central Statistical Administration and as quoted above. The term 'scientist' will be used in the usual English sense of a natural scientist who is engaged, at least part of the time, in fundamental research. 'Technologist' will be used to identify those primarily engaged in the development of new products and processes, the bulk of whom are classified under the rubric 'technical sciences' in Soviet statistics. Here it is worth noting that it is common for scientists to be engaged in both fundamental and applied research and that it is by no means always clear where the boundary between the two should be drawn. Finally the term 'scholar' will be used to refer to those engaged in teaching and research in the humanities and social sciences, in order to describe the non-scientific academic staff of institutions, such as the USSR Academy of Sciences and the universities, in which many different disciplines are represented.

In the Soviet Union teaching and research are separated to a degree not generally found in academic institutions in Great Britain and North America. Whereas much fundamental research is undertaken by universities in the West, this is not generally the case in the USSR. Although the Universities of Moscow and Leningrad (and a number of others) have considerable research commitments, fundamental research in the natural and social sciences is concentrated in the research establishments of the USSR Academy of Sciences and the academies of sciences of the 14 non-Russian republics.

This does not mean that the academies carry out no applied research or development work at all. The USSR Academy of Sciences, for example, is obliged by its statute to conduct some technically orientated research and, like the other academies, is deeply involved in projects of this kind. However, the statute also stipulates that, as its first responsibility, the USSR Academy of Sciences must carry out 'the development of research in the leading directions (*napravleniya*) of the natural and social sciences' which it is charged with supervising wherever such research is conducted, irrespective of the departmental subordination of the institutions concerned.[7] What distinguishes the USSR Academy of Sciences and those of the union republics from the other elements of the Soviet research and higher educational systems is their special responsibility for the conduct of fundamental research and the concentration of staff and resources in them for this purpose. As can be seen in Table 2.1, about 60 per cent of the scientific workers employed in the USSR and union republican academies in recent years have been physicists, mathematicians, chemists, biologists or geologists, whilst the remainder have been engaged either in the humanities and social sciences or in technology.

The traditional commitment of the USSR Academy of Sciences to fundamental research in the natural and social sciences was strengthened as a result of reforms introduced in the early 1960s. Following the publication of a decree by the party and the government in April 1961, virtually all the USSR Academy of Sciences' technically orientated research establishments were transferred to the jurisdiction of appropriate industrial ministries.[8] Over the next two years the USSR Academy of Sciences lost over 80 of its 241 scientific establishments and nearly 2000 of its scientific workers.[9] Two years later a further decree reorganised the management structure of the USSR Academy and extended the transfer of technically orientated research establishments to the academies of sciences of the 14 union republics.[10] By the end of 1963 the combined staffs of the republican academies had also been reduced by some 2000, and 106 establishments had been transferred mainly to the research and development systems of the industrial ministries.[11]

TABLE 2.1 *Scientific workers employed in the USSR and republican academies of sciences by discipline in 1972 (end of year)*

Discipline	Number	Per cent
All	79 918	100.0
Physics and mathematics	19 493	24.4 ⎫
Chemistry	11 847	14.8 ⎪
Biology	11 526	14.4 ⎬ 59.3
Geology and minerology	4 574	5.7 ⎭
Technology	13 206	16.5
History	4 874	6.1
Economics	4 488	5.6
Philosophy	1 349	1.7
Philology	3 919	4.9
Geography	1 459	1.8
Law	520	0.7
Education	105	0.1
Art	348	0.4
Architecture	70	0.1
Medicine	698	0.9
Agriculture	1 214	1.5
Veterinary science	24	0.03
Pharmacy	66	0.1

SOURCE *Vestnik statistiki*, no. 4 (1974) p. 91.

Whilst these reforms clearly shifted the balance of research conducted in the academies of sciences further in the direction of fundamental investigations, their applied role was never abandoned and a responsibility to identify and encourage the development of the technical possibilities arising from basic scientific advances was retained. Rather than diminishing, this applied role has tended to expand during the intervening 20 years, reflecting the emphasis the Communist Party leaders have placed on raising the efficiency of research and development and on increasing the sophistication of Soviet technology. According to a survey carried out among scientific workers employed in the USSR and union republican academies of sciences in recent years, 43.5 per cent of the respondents identified their research as fundamental, 43.4 per cent as applied and 10.5 per cent as a combination of the two.[12] The proportion engaged in fundamental research was higher in the institutes of the USSR Academy than the overall figures but, at 50 per cent, it is clear how misleading it would be to regard the USSR Academy of Sciences as exclusively concerned with this type of research just because most of the Soviet fundamental research effort is concentrated in its institutes.

NATURAL SCIENTISTS AS AN ACADEMIC ELITE

The statute of the USSR Academy of Sciences identifies it as the Soviet Union's leading scientific establishment.[13] This formal status is borne out by the reputations enjoyed by the Academy's central institutes and by the exclusiveness and high qualifications of its scientific staff. To a lesser degree this is also the case with important institutes in the academies of the union republics. This does not mean that there are no well-regarded institutions, involved to some degree with fundamental research, outside the academies of sciences. When one considers establishments like the Karpov Chemical Institute it is clearly the case that prestigious research institutes also exist outside the networks of the academies of sciences. However, assessments of the status of leading branch institutes such as this often take the form of pointing out how similar they are to 'Academy' institutes, and thus reaffirm the USSR Academy of Sciences' national standing.[14]

In spite of having expanded from a staff of about 6000 scientific workers in the immediate post-war years to almost 50 000 today, the USSR Academy of Sciences has remained relatively small and exclusive when considered in the context of the enormous modern Soviet research and development system. As Table 2.2 shows, the number of scientific workers employed in the USSR and union republican academies of sciences, now approaching 100 000, falls some way short of 10 per cent of the total number of scientific workers in the Soviet Union today. Even when the academies of sciences were expanding very rapidly during the 1950s, they never accounted for much more than 12 per cent of the Soviet scientific establishment, and in the early 1960s their staffs fell, in absolute terms, at the time when Soviet scientific manpower was expanding at an unprecedented rate.

TABLE 2.2   *Relative size and growth of the USSR and republican academies of sciences 1950–80 (end of year except where indicated†)*

Year	All scientific workers	Scientific workers in the USSR Academy of Sciences	Scientific workers in the republican academies of sciences	Scientific workers in USSR and republican academies of sciences as % of all scientific workers
1950	162 500†	6 053		
1955	223 893†	13 009†	7 993†	9.4
1960	354 158	23 771	19 057	12.1
1965	664 600		25 450	
1970	927 700	34 788	35 980	7.6
1975	1 223 400	41 836	45 361	7.1
1980	1 373 300	47 825	49 083	7.1

† 1 October

SOURCES   *Bol'shaya Sovetskaya Entsiklopediya*, no. 1 (1949) pp. 570–1; Alexander Vucinich, *The Soviet Academy of Sciences*, Stanford University Press (1956) p. 1; *Kul'turnoe stroitel'stvo SSSR* (Moscow: Gosstatizdat, 1956) pp. 248–9; *Narodnoe khozyaistvo SSSR v 1960g* (Moscow: Gosstatizdat, 1961) p. 787; *Narodnoe obrazovanie, nauka i kul'tura v SSSR* (Moscow: Statistika, 1971) pp. 245–6; *Narodnoe obrazovanie, nauka i kul'tura v SSSR* (Moscow: Statistika, 1977) pp. 299–301; *Narodnoe khozyaistvo SSSR v 1980g* (Moscow: Finansy i Statistika, 1981) pp. 96–7.

During the 1960s the total number of Soviet scientific workers increased from 354 158 to 927 700.[15] The most important contribution to this increase resulted from the expansion of the technical sciences which grew by a factor of three during the decade, by the end of which scientific workers in these disciplines totalled 410 000.[16] However, as a result of the reforms of the early sixties, the size of this category of scientific worker was much reduced in the academies of sciences and they were only marginally affected by the tremendous subsequent expansion of the technical sciences.

During the 1970s the overall rate of increase of scientific manpower slowed considerably and, since then, there has been a certain amount of concern about the problems bequeathed by a decade of very rapid growth. Prominent among these has been the declining quality of Soviet scientific workers. This fell markedly, at least when measured in terms of the proportion of those in possession of a higher degree, especially in those areas, like the technical sciences, which experienced the most rapid growth.

In the USSR higher degrees come in two forms, the *kandidat nauk*, or candidate of sciences and the *doktor nauk*, or doctor of sciences. The candidate of sciences is awarded for a successful public defence of original research, presented in the form of a dissertation, before the academic council of an approved higher educational establishment or research institute. It is generally considered to be roughly equivalent to an American or British PhD but the process whereby it is awarded is more protracted. The doctor of sciences is awarded after a similar public defence but only for work considered to be of substantial significance, which is generally interpreted to mean opening up a new area or, in Soviet terms, 'direction' (*napravlenie*), of investigation or theorising.[17] The recipients of the Soviet doctoral degree are often mature and sometimes even elderly scientists or scholars, who have accumulated a body of work worthy of consideration.

The award of these degrees has to be confirmed by the USSR Higher Attestation Commission which is universally referred to by its Russian acronym, VAK, and was once described to the author as the 'artery of Soviet science' since it governs the flow and direction of those qualified for advancement in the hierarchies of the institutions which compose the Soviet science system. Confirmation of the award of a higher degree by VAK is not automatic and in 1974 its procedures were tightened up as a result of a major reform.[18]

During the 1960s the proportion of scientific workers who had been awarded a higher degree declined sharply from nearly 40 per cent in

TABLE 2.3 A comparison of the proportion of scientific workers holding higher degrees among all scientific workers, those employed in the USSR Academy of Sciences and those employed in the republican academies of sciences, 1950–80 (in per cent) (end of year figures except where indicated†)

Year	All scientific workers	Scientific workers in the USSR Academy of Sciences	Scientific workers in the republican academies of sciences
1950	33	56	
1955	39†	48†	54†
1960	31†		
1965	22		
1970	27	48	41
1975	29	53	45
1980	32	56	48

† 1 October

SOURCES *Bol'shaya Sovetskaya Entsiklopediya*, no. 1 (1949) pp. 570–1; *Kul'turnoe stroitel'stvo SSSR* (Moscow: Gosstatizdat, 1956) p. 249; *Narodnoe khozyaistvo SSSR v 1960g* (Moscow: Gosstatizdat, 1961) p. 784; *Narodnoe obrazovanie, nauka i kul'tura v SSSR* (Moscow: Statistika, 1971) pp. 252–3; *Narodnoe obrazovanie, nauka i kul'tura v SSSR* (Moscow: Statistika, 1977) pp. 299–301; *Narodnoe khozyaistvo SSSR v 1980g* (Moscow: Finansy i Statistika, 1981) pp. 96–7.

1955 to a little over 20 per cent ten years later.[19] This trend affected all disciplines but the decline was steepest where growth had been fastest. By the end of 1965 only a little over 12 per cent of those in the technical sciences had higher degrees, in comparison to 37 per cent a decade earlier. The standard of scientists in mathematics and physics, which were also areas of considerable expansion in these years, suffered too. But, as can be seen from Table 2.3, the overall quality of scientific workers employed in the academies of sciences declined much less sharply than in the country as a whole. By the early 1970s no one discipline had been allowed to fall behind in the academies, whilst the proportion of those in possession of at least the candidate of sciences was considerably greater for each discipline represented in the academies of sciences than was the case for the discipline as a whole.

NATURAL SCIENTISTS AS MEMBERS OF ECONOMIC AND POLITICAL ELITES

Economic status

Whereas 40 years ago Soviet specialists earned more than twice the average wage of industrial workers, today industrial rates have almost caught up completely. The differences between many occupational groups are now less significant than the differences within them. For example, the starting salary of the young specialist after completing higher education is about a quarter of that of a doctor of sciences employed in a research establishment.[20] Writing in the 1970s, Zhores Medvedev stated that senior researchers who did not have higher degrees would have been earning about 120 roubles per month, or about the same as an industrial worker. A senior researcher with the more advanced degree of doctor of sciences would then have been earning upwards of 400 roubles per month, and the director of a research institute about 700 roubles per month. These, incidentally, are the rates of pay received by scientific workers employed by the USSR Academy of Sciences and other leading establishments which have been placed in the first of three categories by which pay scales are determined. Those employed in establishments assigned to the second and third categories received less, perhaps by as much as 200 roubles in the case of an institute director, but probably only marginally less in the case of the most junior posts.[21]

As can be seen from these examples substantial additional payments are forthcoming for the acquisition of higher degrees and academic titles. The emoluments received by a senior scientific researcher with a candidate of sciences degree are almost double those of someone without one. A doctoral degree further boosts income, whilst the titles of corresponding or full member of the USSR Academy of Sciences carry with them additional emoluments of 350 to 500 roubles each month. To take some concrete examples; in recent years a senior scientific worker employed in a research institute of the USSR Academy of Sciences, who possessed a doctorate and who held a part-time professorship at Moscow University, received somewhere in the region of 500 roubles each month or about four times the post's basic salary.[22] The director of a research institute of the USSR Academy of Sciences who was a full member of the USSR Academy earns about 1200 roubles a month, irrespective of other sources of income, which are potentially numerous at this level in the hierarchy.[23] Thus the earnings differential of scientists employed in institutes of the first, most highly remunerated, category has recently been at least of the order of one to ten.

The extent of material inequalities in the Soviet Union is only partially expressed by differences in pay. High rank in any of the civilian or military hierarchies brings with it an assortment of material perquisites which cannot easily be purchased. In addition to high incomes, academicians benefit from access to privileged shops, better housing, superior medical facilities and the provision of dachas and chauffeur-driven cars.[24]

Whilst all this significantly increases the gap between the top and bottom of Soviet hierarchies, there is at least one important privilege from which natural scientists disproportionately benefit irrespectively of rank or title. As the research establishments of the USSR and republican academies of sciences are mostly located in and around Moscow, Leningrad and the larger cities, scientists are more likely than the members of other professions to be able to avoid the material and cultural deprivations associated with provincial life in the Soviet Union.

The Moscow resident's permit is a major prize and its significance for Soviet citizens is hard to exaggerate. In this respect scientific workers are especially favoured, for although they are less concentrated in the capital than used to be the case, still a quarter of the total are employed in Moscow.[25] In the case of the USSR Academy of Sciences, half the scientific workers employed in its establishments work in Moscow.[26] The exceptional magnetism Moscow holds for the Soviet population is a direct reflection of the highly centralised character of the Soviet state and the material and cultural facilities that surround the political elite.

Political status

In a society where almost all economic, cultural and scholarly activity takes place in institutions directly controlled by the state, those holding positions of responsibility in virtually all spheres of employment necessarily become its agents. As the country's leading scientific establishment, the USSR Academy of Sciences is, therefore, required to carry out politico–administrative as well as scientific functions.

In its scientific capacity the USSR Academy functions as the institutional expression of the Soviet scientific community. In its politico–administrative capacity, it is charged with directing the activities of its subordinated research establishments in much the same way as ministries and other organs of the Soviet state, which, like the Academy, are directly responsible to the USSR Council of Ministers for administering various branches of the economy or the provision of services. Beyond this, the USSR Academy of Sciences supervises all important research projects carried out in the natural and social sciences, irrespective of the administrative subordination of the establishments in which they occur. In this respect the USSR Academy of Sciences functions as a kind of super department for fundamental research.[27]

One of the main differences between the USSR Academy of Sciences and ministries or state committees, which emerges from a consideration of its politico-administrative role, is that those occupying its leading positions are elected by, and to some extent answerable to, the full and corresponding members of the Academy who periodically assemble in departmental and general meetings to review policy and to participate in the process of electing new full and corresponding members. Whilst the influence of the Communist Party is not absent from these elections (in fact the party leadership made a specific recommendation when the current president was first elected in 1975), they are unusual in being conducted by secret ballot.[28] In consequence scientific and scholarly opinion has always been reflected in the composition of the USSR Academy of Sciences' leading bodies.

The USSR Academy of Sciences' most important political role is to act as a policy-making and executive body in the natural and social sciences. But the state responsibilities of academicians are not restricted to functions specific to the USSR and republican academies, for a number of them also hold senior positions in other government and party organs. For example, the chairmanship of the State Committee for Science and Technology, the body responsible for the co-ordination of applied research throughout the Soviet Union, is normally held by a full member of the USSR Academy of Sciences. The same is true of the USSR Higher Attestation Commission, which now answers directly to the USSR Council of Ministers, whilst the USSR Ministry of Higher and Secondary Specialised Education is currently headed by a corresponding member of the USSR Academy of Sciences. In the party hierarchy, in recent years, two of those in charge of departments of the apparatus of the Central Committee, the country's most important political bureaucracy, have been full or corresponding members of the Academy. One is Academician S. P. Trapeznikov, who headed the Department of Science and Educational Institutions. The other is Academician Ponamarëv who heads the Central Committee's International Department and is also a candidate member of the Politburo and a secretary of the Central Committee.

Whilst some academicians are deeply involved in research, many others have accumulated heavy administrative responsibilities as they have ascended the academic hierarchy, leaving them little time to supervise the day-to-day running of their institutes. A spectrum of commitments may thus be observed among them, ranging from those who have remained principally concerned with research, through to scientist-administrators, much of whose time is taken up with running the affairs of science, and then on to those whose careers have encompassed much broader political and administrative responsibilities. So, although the USSR Academy of Sciences possesses unique sources of autonomy it is, nevertheless, an organ of the Soviet state and this is naturally reflected in the activities of its full and corresponding members.

The differences in power and influence which exist among scientists elected to, or employed by, the USSR and republican academies of sciences are at least as profound as those of economic status discussed earlier. When speaking of the Soviet scientific community it is necessary to bear in mind that its members occupy vastly different positions in the institutional hierarchy, enabling some to exercise control over the careers of others through the exercise of powers which far exceed those founded on scientific authority alone.

CONCLUSION

The organisation of fundamental research in the Soviet Union is distinguished by the degree to which it is concentrated in the establishments of the USSR Academy of Sciences and, to a lesser extent, in those of the academies of the republics. Although the majority of those employed in these institutions are natural scientists, these bodies are not exclusively concerned with science in the English sense of the word as about a third of their staffs are employed in research in the social sciences and humanities.[29]

In terms of the character of research undertaken in the academies of sciences, it was noted, perhaps surprisingly, that scientists are about equally likely to be engaged in applied as in fundamental investigations. The concentration of the Soviet fundamental research effort in the academies of sciences has not, therefore, precluded their continuing, and almost certainly expanding, involvement in technical work. Here regional variations are evident. For example, the proportion of applied research undertaken in the establishments of the Siberian Division of the USSR Academy of Sciences is noticeably greater than in the central institutes of Moscow and Leningrad. Taken as a whole, the proportion of applied research which occurs in the republican academies is greater than that undertaken in the USSR Academy of Sciences.

There is about a 50 per cent chance that the academy natural scientist will possess a higher degree. Again, this is slightly higher in the USSR Academy of Sciences than those of the republics. Variations are almost certain to exist among the staff of different institutes. It would be surprising if those employed in the most prestigious establishments, such as the Lebedev Physics Institute or the Institute of Physical Problems, were not more highly qualified than the norm.

Almost without exception, the 50 per cent of natural scientists who do not hold a higher degree occupy the relatively minor posts of junior and, sometimes, senior researcher, and receive modest remuneration. Of the 50 per cent with higher degrees, less than one in six have the more advanced doctor of sciences necessary today, at least in the USSR Academy of Sciences, for promotion to the more responsible posts of laboratory chief and above.[30]

It follows that the vast majority of natural scientists do not benefit from the perquisites enjoyed by the elite. Many of the younger ones live with parents and a senior researcher with a growing family who possesses a higher degree will consider him or herself fortunate to occupy a two-roomed flat in one of the giant blocks that dominate the outskirts of most Soviet cities.

However profound the material differences may be between the scientific elite and the scientist at the bench, the relationship is often less distant than that which obtains between the industrial boss and the factory floor. The basic professional equality of scientists can ameliorate the influence of rank, making the scientific hierarchy more responsive to the wishes of the rank and file than those of other state institutions. Nevertheless the USSR Academy of Sciences remains an organ of the Soviet state, and as such presents many opportunities for the development of careers in administration and politics for those who reach the topmost positions. Although the USSR Academy has preserved something of the substance as well as the form of its unusually democratic internal arrangements, the autonomy of its academicians is limited by the presence among their ranks of those who have taken on substantial political and administrative responsibilities in addition to their scientific or scholarly interests.

3 The Educational Background and Social Characteristics of Soviet Natural Scientists

This Chapter completes the task of drawing up a social profile of Soviet natural scientists. To the discussion of their academic, economic and political attributes it adds an analysis of the factors which influence the attainment of a scientific career by Soviet school children. Following this is a description of the way in which Soviet scientists are distributed in terms of age, gender and ethnicity. The chapter concludes with a summary of the characteristics most frequently observed among Soviet natural scientists and some comments on their broader social and political significance.

THE DESIRABILITY OF A SCIENTIFIC CAREER AND THE FACTORS AFFECTING ITS ATTAINMENT

Since empirical social science began to re-emerge in the Soviet Union in the early 1960s, the popularity of science has been consistently demonstrated by surveys conducted to determine the attitudes of school children and students towards different occupations. Respondents have usually been asked to rate the prestige and attractiveness of various professions and the results invariably placed *intelligentsiya* occupations at the top on both counts. In those cases where respondents have been given the opportunity to discriminate between different disciplines, physics, mathematics and medicine have been the most consistently highly rated. Boys have usually shown the strongest attraction to physics and mathematics, whilst girls have tended to rate the medical sciences as, or more, highly.[1]

Although the Soviet higher educational system annually graduates many thousands of students, the channels leading into the prestigious natural science institutes of the academies of sciences are narrow. This is particularly so for those channels feeding the institutes of the USSR Academy of Sciences located in and around Moscow, Leningrad and Novosibirsk. In the first place only about 10 per cent of Soviet students attend universities, in which the teaching of academic subjects is mostly concentrated. The vast majority of Soviet students attend other higher educational establishments. Over 40 per cent of them are enrolled in higher technical institutes, most of which provide a rather narrow training in specialised engineering skills.[2] Even within the academically orientated sector, the quality of the institutions varies a good deal. It is taken for granted in the USSR that if a student has ambitions to become a scientist and to work in an establishment of the USSR Academy of Sciences, it helps immeasurably to have excelled at Moscow, Leningrad or Novosibirsk University, or at one of the central polytechnics or physico-technical institutions, rather than at a more peripheral establishment.

The advantages of being educated in the centre are illustrated by the educational background of full members of the USSR Academy of Sciences. Among those academicians alive in 1970 some 73 per cent had received their diplomas from higher educational establishments either in Moscow or Leningrad; 34 per cent were from Moscow University and 12 per cent from Leningrad University.[3]

Many of the departments in these universities have long established ties with research institutes of the USSR Academy of Sciences. Staff of the Academy have always taught on a part-time basis in Moscow University and in the capital's other leading higher schools. During the 1930s and 1940s the USSR Academy provided students with an opportunity to acquire research experience by bringing them into its laboratories. This, in turn, enabled Academy scientists to do their own talent spotting.[4]

In physics this kind of arrangement was influential in the setting up of the Moscow Physico-Technical and Engineering Physics Institutes. They were founded to provide the USSR Academy of Sciences with a reliable supply of well-prepared researchers, by overcoming the divisions between teaching and research and between fundamental and applied science which have always been characteristic weaknesses of the Soviet higher education system.[5] The seriousness of these defects has been recognised for many years and continues to attract criticism. One suggestion, which appears to have won a fair amount of support recently, favours the setting-up of a number of additional establishments along these lines in order to meet the growing need for well-trained scientists and technologists in other fields such as bio-chemistry and medical cybernetics.[6]

The uneven quality of the Soviet higher educational system is to a considerable degree the legacy of the rapid expansion that occurred during the 1930s. In order to meet the burgeoning demand for technically trained cadres during the industrialisation drive, the higher educational system was required to expand its enrolment before adequately qualified staff could be trained and before the secondary school system had been developed sufficiently to provide a broad stream of properly educated school leavers. Academic entry require-ments were waived for upwardly mobile workers, peasants and Communist Party activists who filled the newly organised higher technical schools, many of which were 'higher' in name only.[7] During these years most of the universities and many other well-established institutions were divided up into more specialised institutes based on their separate faculties. A few of the universities retained their identity as unitary institutions but their combined enrolment fell from over 50 000 to under 10 000 between 1928 and 1932.[8]

One of the legacies of these years is the large number of narrowly specialised engineering institutions lacking the staff and the resources to provide adequate instruction in the scientific foundations of the technical courses they teach. It was this system which was required to cope with massive expansion of the technical sciences during the late 1950s and throughout the 1960s, the longer-term consequences of which have been causing anxiety in the 1970s and 1980s.[9]

Although higher educational opportunities are immensely generous in the USSR, only a small proportion of the institutions are considered to be genuinely prestigious and attractive. Students with academic aspirations do not merely seek a higher education as an end in itself but attempt to discriminate in favour of the relatively few good in-stitutions located in the large cities. In the natural sciences this generally means the appropriate faculties of Moscow, Leningrad or Novosibirsk universities, or one of the broader technical schools like Leningrad Polytechnical Institute or, probably best of all, Moscow Physico-Technical Institute, which takes some diploma as well as postgraduate students.[10]

Success in gaining acceptance at one of the universities or broader institutes is influenced by a number of factors among which home background appears to be the most significant. In spite of efforts to the contrary, the Communist Party has never been able to eradicate the conditions which give rise to the transmission of cultural advantages from one generation to the next.[11] Even in the midst of the proletarianisation drive in the early 1930s, students from non-worker and non-peasant backgrounds still constituted a third of those entering the higher education system.[12] This was in part a consequence of the absence of adequate schools outside the main cities. Urban children with more highly educated and often professional parents were therefore disproportionately well represented, even then, among those who gained entrance to higher educational institutions after the politically determined quotas had been filled.

More recently Soviet sociologists have assembled a great deal of information about the social origins of school children and students which strongly supports the hypothesis that the educational level of parents exerts a powerful influence on the attainment of children. This has been demonstrated by a number of studies, the largest of which was based on a survey involving nearly 50 000 school children and students carried out in 1973–4 in several different regions of the USSR.[13] A comparison of the educational level of parents, measured at various points as their children progressed through the secondary schools and on to the first year of higher education institutions, revealed that the proportion of children from more highly educated backgrounds was significantly greater, both among the first-year students in higher educational establishments and among tenth and final-year school children, than among the children attending the first-year school course. In the case of the first-year school children, 26 per cent of the fathers and 29 per cent of the mothers had secondary specialised or higher education. This had risen to 36 per cent of the fathers and 37 per cent of the mothers by the tenth year and to 54 and 53 per cent respectively by the first-year course of higher education.[14] This study may not fully take account of all regional variations among the Soviet population but the impact of more highly educated home backgrounds on the attainment of children is clearly visible.[15]

This effect becomes particularly marked for those children whose parents had received higher as opposed to only secondary specialised education. Here 32 per cent of the fathers and 27 per cent of the mothers of students attending the first course of higher educational establishments had themselves received higher education. This was between two and three times the percentages registered by the parents of children on the first-year course at school and some five times greater than the percentage of men and women who had received a higher education among the Soviet population as a whole.[16]

While the level of educational attainment of the parents of Soviet students attending higher educational institutions is generally much above the national average, considerable variation has been observed in the educational standard of the parents of students enrolled in different disciplines. Over the years a number of surveys have shown that the largest proportions of students from more highly educated home backgrounds are to be found enrolled in the more academically orientated establishments and, in particular, the universities, as opposed to agricultural, technical and pedagogical institutes. Within the universities the largest proportions of students from more highly educated home backgrounds are to be observed in the natural sciences. This has shown up in studies conducted in and around Sverdlovsk in the 1960s and, more recently, in the various regions of the country covered by the large survey of 50 000 school children and students referred to above.[17] In this study the highest proportions of students from specialist, that is of at least secondary specialist, home backgrounds, were observed in the universities and medical institutes. Registering the highest proportions of all were students attending the natural science faculties of the universities. Here 61 per cent of the fathers and 38 per cent of the mothers had secondary specialised education or better.[18]

Information relating to the background of those taking the next step towards a career as a scientist, that is the postgraduate students, is not nearly so readily available as that concerning school children and undergraduate students. A survey carried out amongst both diploma and postgraduate students in 12 institutes of the USSR Academy of Sciences and 20 higher educational institutions in Leningrad in the late 1960s neither distinguished between discipline nor differentiated between the level of parental education of those classified as coming from non-manual backgrounds. However, the results showed that whereas 57 per cent of the undergraduate students were placed in this category (non-manual occupation or the children of those so employed), this rose to 71 per cent in the case of the postgraduates attending higher educational establishments, and to 73 per cent of those undertaking postgraduate work in the research institutes of the USSR Academy of Sciences.[19] Apparently this last figure had fallen from 88 per cent in 1963. Although no further information was given, the authors of this study remarked that it would be interesting to know the proportion of scientific workers among the parents of postgraduates and thereby gain some idea of the degree to which scientific careers run in families.

Information about those who have advanced the further step and gained employment in research establishments is provided by a study of over 1000 young specialists appended to the large survey of school children and students referred to extensively above. Here the term 'young specialist' was understood to include those who had worked for up to nine years after completing higher education. Young specialists were surveyed in four types of establishments: engineering-technical workers in industrial enterprises, specialists in project and design bureaux, scientists and engineers employed in scientific research institutes serving different branches of industry, and scientists and scientific technical staff employed by research establishments of the USSR Academy of Sciences. With the exception of those employed in the Academy of Sciences, respondents were taken from establishments in both Moscow and Voronezh. In the case of the USSR Academy of Sciences, 101 scientists were surveyed in the Institute of Organic and Analytical Chemistry in Moscow.

Comparisons between these groups of highly-trained specialists revealed interesting differences in terms of social and educational backgrounds and levels of academic attainment. Whilst the respondents from all four types of establishment registered disproportionately highly in terms of those from specialist home backgrounds, there was considerable variation among them. This ranged from 37 per cent in the case of engineers working in industry to 70 per cent in the case of scientists employed by the USSR Academy of Sciences. In terms of the young specialists' educational backgrounds, whereas 59 per cent of the Academy scientists had attended university, the vast majority of specialists in other categories had attended polytechnics and higher technical schools. With respect to academic attainment, 84 per cent of the young Academy scientists had received the highest grade of 'excellent' (*otlichno*) on completing their higher education, in comparison to less than 50 per cent for the respondents employed in each of the three other categories of establishment.[20]

AGE, GENDER AND ETHNICITY

Age

The average age of Soviet scientific workers increased as a result of the casualties among young people incurred during the Second World War, but with the rapid increase in the number of scientific workers, beginning in the late 1950s and continuing during the 1960s, it began to fall. Between the censuses of 1939 and 1959 the proportion of scientific workers below the age of 40 declined from 66 per cent to 55 per cent but, by 1966, 64 per cent were 40 or under.[21] As the growth rate stabilised during the late 1960s and early 1970s, so the process of rejuvenation came to a halt. By 1972, 63 per cent of all scientific workers were 40 or younger, as compared with 66 per cent of those employed in the establishments of the USSR and republican academies of science at the time.[22]

More precise and recent information is available for natural scientists employed in the academies of sciences but this is not comparable with the figures quoted in the previous paragraph, as it is based on a sample which includes postgraduate students and pro- bationer researchers (*stazhëry*), excluded from the category of scientific workers as defined by the Central Statistical Administration. Accordingly a rather higher proportion, some 73 per cent of the surveyed scientists, were found to be under 40 and over half of them under 35. Of greater interest, however, are the age distributions given in this survey for scientists classified according to their seniority in the academic hierarchy. Among those scientists in charge of research establishments 26 per cent were under 40, whilst 30 per cent were 55 or over. A similar distribution was found for those placed in the next category down, with 28 per cent of heads of laboratories being below 40 and 26 per cent having reached the age of 50 or exceeded it. Over 50 per cent of senior researchers holding the degree of doctor of sciences were 55 years old or over whilst 21 per cent were under 40 and 5 per cent under 35.[23]

Although the proportion of younger scientific workers employed in the academies of sciences who hold higher degrees is greater than the national figure, the evidence suggests that the natural sciences have not remained immune from the widely recognised problem of increasing age among more senior and highly qualified Soviet scientific workers.

Gender

Over the past 30 years the proportion of women among scientific workers has registered a gradual increase from about 36 per cent in the 1950s to just under 40 per cent in the late 1970s and early 1980s.[24] But the proportion drops sharply among those holding higher degrees and more senior posts. About 28 per cent of those holding the candidate of sciences degree are women, as are about 14 per cent of doctors of sciences. Only some 3 per cent of full and corresponding members of the various academies and those with the title of professor are female.[25]

The USSR and republican academies of sciences are no exception to this overall pattern. The main difference here requiring comment is that, according to survey data, the overall proportion of women is higher in these establishments, at about 43 per cent, than in the Soviet scientific system as a whole.[26]

The proportion of men and women in the USSR and republican academies of sciences does not reflect a uniform distribution throughout the various research institutions which compose them but tends to vary according to region and age group. Whilst the proportion of men increases in some of the more peripheral establishments, it decreases in the central research establishments of Moscow and Leningrad, where the proportion of women is reported to exceed the overall figure of 43 per cent. The distribution of men and women among different age groups bears a close relationship to the relative attrition of women which occurs as the academic hierarchy is ascended. Whereas some 68 per cent of natural scientists in the academies of sciences below the age of 25 are women, males predominate in all subsequent age groups with the exception of those 55 years of age or over.[27]

The proportion of women falls most sharply in those age ranges, the late twenties and early thirties, when the demands of the traditional division of labour in child rearing falls most heavily upon them. As this period coincides with the time when higher degrees are being prepared and more responsibilities sought, it is perhaps surprising that as many as 50 per cent of scientists currently receiving the degree of candidate of sciences in the academies of sciences are reported to be women. It would appear, however, that women take longer to complete the candidate's degree and that many do not succeed in submitting their doctoral theses at all. As the possession of the doctor of sciences is now virtually a prerequisite for promotion to posts with administrative responsibilities it is not surprising that the proportion of women among the heads of laboratories in the academies of sciences is said to amount to between 20 and 30 per cent.[28]

Among the explanations advanced for the disproportionately low representation of women in the more senior scientific posts, the unequal distribution of domestic burdens is clearly of great importance. It has, however, been pointed out that the overwhelming prevalence of men at the very top of the academic hierarchy (in 1980 only three of the full members of the USSR Academy of Sciences were women) both sustains male solidarity and reduces the power of women to take steps to bring about a fairer system.[29]

Ethnicity

As far as the ethnic composition of Soviet scientific workers is concerned, Russians clearly dominate. In 1975 Russians accounted for 818 246 of the 1 223 428 scientific workers recorded in that year. Following the Russians, at some distance, were the Ukrainians with 134 243 scientific workers and the Jews with 69 374.[30] Of these three, the Russians and the Jews were among the major ethnic groups which are most over-represented among Soviet scientific workers. Russians constituted some 52 per cent of the Soviet population yet accounted for some 67 per cent of scientific workers; Jews constituted less than 1 per cent of the population but nearly 6 per cent of scientific workers. Other over-represented nationalities included the Armenians, Georgians, Latvians and Estonians, but all of these were over-represented to a much smaller extent than either the Russians or the Jews.[31]

Some idea of the historical significance of the role played by Jews in Soviet intellectual life is suggested by the fact that, in spite of the extent of their statistical over-representation, the proportion of Jews among scientific workers has been falling for over 40 years. It has been estimated that in 1939 nearly 20 per cent of Soviet scientific workers were Jewish.[32] By 1959 this had been halved, and further declined to 7 per cent in 1970, 6 per cent in 1973 and just below 6 per cent in 1975.[33] A breakdown by nationality of Soviet postgraduate students during the early 1970s may indicate one of the means by which this decline has been sustained in recent years. Whereas the total number of postgraduate students hardly changed between 1970 and 1973, the number of Jewish postgraduates among them fell by nearly 1500, or by 30 per cent.[34] In consequence it would appear that restricted opportunities for postgraduate work may have been one of the more important factors contributing to the decline in the proportion of Jews among Soviet scientific workers in recent years.

CONCLUSION: A SOCIAL PROFILE OF SOVIET NATURAL SCIENTISTS

There would clearly be little value in constructing a synthetic 'average' Soviet scientist but, on the basis of the foregoing, it is possible to identify some of the characteristics most likely to be encountered amongst the staff of research establishments, in addition to those relating to academic qualifications and economic and political status discussed in the previous chapter.

In terms of educational and social background, the academy scientist has most probably been born in a large city, come from an educated home and attended a city school. Following school he or she is likely to have attended a university rather than one of the other kinds of higher educational institution and, on completing the course, to have attained the highest grades. But whereas the broadest paths into the institutes of the USSR Academy of Sciences lead through the universities of Moscow, Leningrad and, more recently, Novosibirsk, the universities of many of the capitals of the republics also function as similar channels feeding their respective academies.

It was also observed that the level of education of parents greatly influences the chances of a child becoming a natural scientist. This becomes more pronounced as each stage of the educational process is traversed. The evidence suggests that a significant proportion of the Soviet intelligentsia reproduces itself as cultural advantages are handed from one generation to the next. Of relevance here is the fact that without any highly paid occupations to be found, at least legally, outside state employment, the higher educational system plays an even more crucial role in determining career opportunities in the USSR than in western countries.

With regard to differences of age, sex and ethnic identity, the majority of academy scientists are under 40 years old, male, and belong to the nationalities prevailing in the republic of their respective academy of sciences.

Whilst the vast majority of young scientists occupy the more junior posts, those in their early thirties form a significant proportion, some 15 per cent, of the heads of establishments and laboratories. Here there are certain to be significant differences between disciplines, for it is known that there are quite wide divergences with respect to the average ages of recipients of higher degrees, the prerequisite for promotion. One would, therefore, expect to find relatively more young people occupying senior posts in mathematically-based disciplines, where higher degrees are generally gained earlier, than in the other sciences.[35]

The proportion of male and female scientists varies according to age, hierarchical position, geographical location and discipline. Male predominance is greatest among scientists in their early thirties and early fifties, in the more senior posts and in the more peripheral regions. Whilst comprehensive data is absent, sociological investigations have demonstrated that women predominate in the Leningrad institutes of biological and chemical profiles of the USSR Academy of Sciences, whereas men prevail in physics and mathematics.[36]

The ethnic composition of the academies of sciences is obviously related to the prevailing nationalities of the republics concerned. There are, however, considerable differences between republics in terms of the extent to which their indigenous populations are represented among the scientific workers employed in research and higher educational establishments. For example, nearly 95 per cent of the scientific workers employed in Armenia are Armenians but less than 30 per cent of those employed in Kazakhstan are Kazakhs. Except in the cases of the Ukraine and Belorussia, where a good deal of mixing with Russians has occurred, the lower percentages of indigenous scientific workers are generally to be observed in the less industrially developed republics of Soviet Central Asia. In contrast, the higher educational and research institutions of those republics with long-established intellectual traditions in the Caucasus and the Baltic, for example, tend to be dominated by scientific workers of indigenous nationality.[37]

With respect to the USSR Academy of Sciences there can be little doubt that Russians predominate, whilst Jews form a significant minority. However, here it should be remembered that the USSR Academy of Sciences employs about the same number of scientific workers as the 14 non-Russian academies combined.

In spite of the intrusion of non-academic criteria in the selection processes leading to careers in the Soviet academic system, science has, nevertheless, provided an avenue to a worthwhile career in which political criteria exercise much less influence than elsewhere. Although no statistics are available, it is widely believed among Soviet intellectuals that one of the main attractions of a career in academic life, and especially in the natural sciences, is the relative insulation it affords from political involvement. This, together with the importance of education in Jewish culture, goes a long way to explaining why so many Soviet natural scientists have always been Jewish, and why the effects of discrimination in this particular sphere are so sharply felt by the Jewish community in the USSR. It also marks out a career in science as unique in the sense that the intensity of party control exercised in other areas regarded as important by the political leadership does not obtain to the same extent in science.

4 Soviet Scientists and World Science: The Effectiveness and Social Relations of Soviet Natural Scientists

The previous chapters dealt with scientists as one of the occupational categories into which the Soviet working population is divided. This chapter is concerned with Soviet scientists as members of real professional groups. It considers how Soviet scientists organise themselves and how effectively they contribute to the advancement of their disciplines in the world at large.

The relationship between these two questions, the one concerned with the social relations and the other with the effectiveness of scientists, may be clarified by reflecting upon the features which distinguish the natural sciences from other kinds of empirical knowledge and cultural expression. Whilst the natural sciences differ among themselves in terms of the comprehensiveness and explanatory power of their theories, they may be distinguished from other forms of knowledge by the precision with which their concepts are defined and the replicability of their experimental procedures.[1] These are essential conditions for the achievement by scientists of levels of agreement about what may be regarded as known and knowable in their respective disciplines, which are unattainable in less exact branches of knowledge. In the social sciences, for example, concepts are almost invariably open to a wide variety of interpretations. Generally conditions for the testing of hypotheses are unamenable to the kind of control necessary for the accumulation of knowledge of sufficient reliability to provide a basis for the kind of intellectual consensus found among natural scientists.[2]

It is the capacity of scientists to agree upon assumptions and to focus their energies on what are regarded as solvable problems that is widely considered to be an important component in explanations of the rapid and sustained accumulation of knowledge which has distinguished the development of the natural sciences since the seventeenth century.[3] However, the capacity for generating progress through intellectual agreement cannot be understood purely in terms of the disinterested pursuit of knowledge without ignoring other prominent aspects of the professional relations of scientists. The frequency of instances when scientists have arrived at the same findings simultaneously is hard to explain without reference to intellectual consensus,[4] but the associated disputes over priority, which also pepper the history of the natural sciences, cannot be easily understood without also recognising the importance of proprietary and competitive feelings among scientists.[5] Knowledge may be shared, but individual contributions are distinctly labelled and are made in the expectation that they will be publicly acknowledged by those seeking to build upon them.

The social and cognitive aspects of science are thus inextricably linked. Recognition by professional peers is both a criterion of the significance of research results and an incentive for pursuing further work. As the mechanism through which these processes are effected, scientific communities play crucial roles in influencing the direction of research, establishing its value and distributing professional authority, even though they lack the stability and official authority of the institutions in which research is actually carried out.

THE ANALYSIS OF SCIENCE BY MEANS OF CITATIONS

A useful way of studying the changing relationship between the structure of science and the behaviour of scientists is by observing the interconnection in quantitative terms of the bibliographic references, or citations, made by authors to the published literature from which their own contributions draw. The choice involved in citing one article, rather than another, expresses a judgement about its relative merits by the author of the later article in which the reference occurs. Citation is, therefore, both an aspect of the many-faceted relationship that grows up among scientists and, at the same time, an expression of the value assigned by scientists to the papers published in their disciplines.

Working from the very large population of papers made available as a result of the publication of the Science Citation Index (SCI), and treating each one as a unit of knowledge, Derek de Solla Price was able to examine the relationships which exist among them.[6] He observed that each paper carries an average of about a dozen citations back to past literature, the analysis of which revealed two contrasting styles of citation. The first, accounting for about half the citations, consisted of a patternless set of connections between new papers and the entire body of older papers published in any particular field. But the other half of the references was quite different. They connected back to a relatively small number of highly interrelated recent papers:

In a particular field each recent paper is connected to all its neighbors by many lines of citation. A convenient image of the pattern is to be found in knitting. Each stitch is strongly attached to the previous row and to all its neighbors. To extend the analogy, sometimes a stitch is dropped and the knitted strip separates into different rows, each one of them a new subfield descended from the first.[7]

This structured style of citation Price called 'research-front' to distinguish it from the patternless type which he referred to as 'archival'.

Using this analogy Price was able to clarify the way in which new papers are related to older ones and thus derive an explanation of the sustained exponential growth of science when measured in terms of any of the more readily quantifiable indicators, whether money, manpower or, as in this case, scientific papers.[8] Since every scientific paper to be published produces, on average, one citation per year, and since it takes about 12 citations to make one new paper, this represents a growth rate of 8 per cent per year, or a doubling of the number of published research papers every 10 years, which is consistent with other attempts to estimate the rate at which science grows. The key to understanding the rapidity of the growth of science, in terms of Price's 'knitting' analogy, is the process whereby very recent knowledge breeds new knowledge so much more quickly than does older knowledge which has become packed down in the archive. It is the interrelated structure and regular but rapid growth from the surface which Price has shown, through the analysis of citations, to distinguish science from the literature of non-scientific scholarship.

THE RELATIVE EFFECTIVENESS OF SOVIET SCIENTISTS AS SHOWN BY CITATIONS

Price's analysis of citations attracted the attention of Soviet scholars during the 1960s when the study of science, from the point of view of the social sciences, was gaining momentum in the USSR. The most systematically conducted analyses of citations were carried out by a group of Soviet scholars drawn from a variety of disciplines, two of whom, V. V. Nalimov and Z. M. Mul'chenko, published a book entitled *Naukometriya* ('Scienceometrics'), which remains one of the most informative contributions to emerge from the USSR.[9]

In this book, the authors set out to compare the effectiveness of the contributions made to world science by scientists publishing in a number of principal scientific nations in a variety of disciplines. The countries chosen were the United States, the Soviet Union, the United Kingdom, France and the two Germanies. The disciplines for which data were assembled were mathematical statistics, physical and analytical chemistry, metallurgy and three areas selected from the biological sciences. In each case the source of the data was either the main Soviet or American reference journal or the principal journal published in each country in each discipline. Their procedure consisted of two stages. The first established the volume of contributions made by authors publishing in each discipline in each country. The second was designed to measure the effectiveness of each national contribution by comparing the proportion of citations received by the published articles of each country's scientists in the articles appearing in journals published in other countries.

In terms of the volume of published papers the combined contributions of the USA and the UK were the greatest, accounting, as a rule, for about 55 per cent of the total. Next came the Soviet Union, generally accounting for some 20 per cent. The remaining countries followed a considerable distance behind. When it came to comparing the weight of contributions, in terms of articles published, with the effectiveness of these contributions (measured by the citations they attracted from scientists publishing in foreign journals), considerable variations were revealed among the various countries.

In the case of Anglo-American authors they found that the level of citation of their work by authors publishing in foreign journals matched the effort expended on publications. These scientists contributed about 55 per cent of the total number of articles published in each field and received about 55 per cent of all the citations listed by foreign authors. The only exception to this rule was the USSR in whose journals Anglo-American papers were less frequently cited, but they still accounted for between 25 and 30 per cent of citations.

There was a gross discrepancy, however, between the level of citations made of the work of Soviet scientists by authors publishing in the journals of other countries and the Soviet effort in terms of articles published. Whereas the USSR contributed some 20 per cent of articles it usually received only some 3 to 4 per cent, and never more than 6 per cent, of the total citations of authors writing in non-Soviet journals.[10] Soviet authors were, therefore, citing Anglo-American articles six or seven times more frequently than their own were being cited by scientists publishing in the USA or the UK.

The findings of the Soviet investigators are supported by two studies carried out by Western scholars. The first, by Narin and Carpenter, is a comprehensive inquiry covering all the main disciplines of the natural sciences together with psychology, clinical medicine and engineering.[11] The second is a more specialised study of the quality of polymer research in the USSR carried out by Arthur Holt.[12]

The source of data used by Narin and Carpenter is a set of 492 journals selected from the SCI covering several years between 1965 and 1972. To this was added a subset of all the journals, 2143 in all, covered by the SCI in 1972. Like the Soviet investigators, Narin and Carpenter first established a country-by-discipline count of publications, thereby establishing the weight of national contributions. Here they used more precise indicators than the Soviet scholars, enabling them to assign journals fractionally among disciplines and identify authors' nationalities by the location of the institutions in which they worked, rather than by the nationality of the journal in which the article was published. Precautions were also taken to compensate for the bias towards the inclusion of a disproportionately large number of American journals in the SCI. This was achieved by substituting the specialised abstracting journal, or augmenting the SCI data in the disciplines affected in this way.

In general the publication counts showed the USA occupying the leading positions, followed by the USSR some way behind, followed a long way behind by the UK and Germany and then by Japan and France. The USA was pre-eminent in the volume of publications in physics and geophysics, molecular biology, systematic biology, psychology and engineering and shared pre-eminence with the USSR in mathematics, chemistry and metallurgy.

As in the Soviet study, a count of the number of citations made to the 492 journals composing the first set was undertaken to see if the ratios of the number of citations to the number of publications would indicate differences in the influence, or effectiveness, of national publications. To accomplish this a citation-to-publication ratio was established to measure the relative frequency of citation to a given country, in a given discipline, in a given year.[13]

The results showed that the USA and the UK were almost always the leaders when assessed in terms of this ratio, indicating a citation preference for the publications of the two English-speaking countries. The pattern of citation to publication for the USSR varied from reasonably high in mathematics, physics and geophysics, to strikingly low in chemistry and metallurgy. It was suggested that these differences might be due to variations in the amount of translated Soviet material available in different disciplines.

In order to examine the possibility that the sample of publications selected might reflect the heavy proportion of publications from the USA and the UK in the SCI, and thus be the cause of the high citation to publication ratios associated with these countries, Narin and Carpenter went on to analyse the more detailed information contained in their 1972 subset. Only for this year do the data contain the *source* of citations by both country and journal.

The resulting analysis showed three different kinds of finding. The first presented the measurement of citations to publications of the USA by the other countries in each discipline. The second showed the citation occurring within each country and the third, and in this context the most interesting, showed the measurement of 'outside-of-country' citation for each country in each discipline.

The conclusions drawn from these findings may be summarised as follows. The relative positions of the USA and the UK are very high, with the USA being particularly highly cited by the outside world. Here the Soviet Union is an exception, for Soviet authors, whilst substantially citing US publications, cite them a good deal less in almost all disciplines than do other non-American authors.[14]

As might be anticipated, the figures on the occurrence of citation within each of the countries showed that scientists are a good deal more likely to cite the work of their fellow-countrymen than that of foreign scientists. However, when it comes to the measurement of the level of 'outside-of-country' citation for each country in each discipline, the USA came out highest in all disciplines except for one. This contrasts dramatically with the position of the USSR which received by far the fewest citations from the outside world, usually by quite considerable magnitudes. Narin and Carpenter summarise their findings in the following way:

> For citations, the relative positions of the United States and the United Kingdom are very high, with the US particularly highly cited by the outside world. France and Soviet Union are generally very low, with the Soviet Union getting especially few citations from the outside world.[15]

The second Western study, carried out by Arthur Holt, concentrates on one particular area of chemistry. It is especially useful in this context because it analyses the citations contained in a selection of six leading East European chemical journals as well as in journals published in the Soviet Union, Western Europe and the United States. The East European journals were included in order to assess the relative standing of polymer research in the USSR from what was considered to be a less partial standpoint than might have been the case if only Soviet and Western journals had been used. As the author points out, East European scientists have traditional ties with the West, which they attempt to maintain, but the political links with the Soviet Union engender closer relations with the Soviet scientists and eases accessibility to their work.

The inquiry showed that whilst the citations made by Soviet authors contain a high proportion of Western publications, this is not reciprocated by Western scientists. The discrepancy was so considerable that it remained clearly visible even after the figures for the citation to Soviet work had been multiplied by a factor of two-and-a-half in order compensate for the difference in the size of the population in the USSR and the Western countries considered in this study.

The analysis of the East European journals showed two patterns of citation. In four of the six journals Western work predominated, even after allowing for differences in population. The two remaining journals, although on balance more inclined towards the West, were more orientated towards Soviet work. It was observed that unlike the other journals, which were primarily concerned with fundamental research, these two dealt, to a greater extent, with work of an applied or technical kind, more open to influences arising outside science and thus more likely to reflect national differences. Also, one of these two journals contained an abnormally high proportion of Soviet contributions, which resulted in a disproportionately large number of citations to Soviet publications.

The overall picture of the citations from East European journals is that in fundamental research they rate the West considerably more highly than the Soviet Union, while in applied research the West is still rated more highly, but the gap is not so great.[16]

The conclusion which can be reached on the basis of Holt's analysis of Soviet, Western and East European journals is that his findings are consistent with those of Nalimov and Mul'chenko, and Narin and Carpenter. That is, there is a definite pattern of low citation of Soviet work by non-Soviet scientists.

To the assessment of Soviet scientific performance based on the analysis of citations may be added a number of other judgements which have been made over the years. Conspicuous among these have been the efforts of a few Soviet natural scientists to draw attention to weaknesses they perceived in the Soviet scientific system. Zhores Medvedev has recounted how, many years ago, he developed a number of indices in order to compare the effectiveness of bio-chemical research in the Soviet Union and the USA. These included counting the number of journals and papers published by each country, comparing the rapidity with which papers appeared in print, assessing the sophistication of research techniques and several other indicators. At the time Medvedev did not attempt to publish his findings because they proved to be so detrimental to the Soviet Union.[17]

A little later, in 1965, Pyotr Kapitsa claimed, in a report to the General Meeting of the USSR Academy of Sciences, that in spite of rough parity in the number of scientists, the Soviet Union published about half as many articles as the USA.[18] Subsequently attention has been drawn to the embarrassingly small number of Nobel Prizes won by Soviet scientists.[19]

Although often couched in vague and euphemistic terms, a similar message may be discerned in the work of some Soviet social scientists. This is particularly clear when evidence is being provided to illustrate the urgency of pursuing official policy which seeks to effect a transfer from the extensive to the intensive use of resources invested in science. An unacceptable discrepancy between the effort expended on science and the output attained is thus recognised in Soviet science policy and by its official interpreters.[20]

It may be concluded that studies of citations have provided a means of systematically conducting comprehensive comparisons of the scientific performances of different nations. As such, they have introduced a valuable new dimension into attempts to assess the effectiveness of the Soviet scientific system which, for many years, has been thought to be falling below what might have been expected from it. However, the usefulness of citations extends beyond comparisons of research performance. As citations are also one of the many strands by which scientists are linked, studying their structure can be helpful in clarifying how scientists of different countries communicate with each other and form networks and organise themselves into groups. It is these questions with which the rest of this chapter is primarily concerned.

THE SOCIAL RELATIONS OF SOVIET SCIENTISTS: CLUES FROM THE EXPLANATIONS OF THE LEVEL OF SOVIET RESEARCH PERFORMANCE

The communication problem

A useful source of information bearing on the social organisation of Soviet natural scientists is to be found among the explanations which have been advanced to account for the relative weakness of scientific research in the USSR. Scholars differ over the degree of significance which should be assigned to a number of factors, prominent among which are the intellectual and social isolation of Soviet scientists, the inferiority of Soviet scientific equipment, and the questionable quality of Soviet scientists. Explanations which stress the first of these are of the most immediate use as a source of clues about the kind of social relationships characteristic of Soviet scientists.

As exponents of this first type of explanation, Nalimov and Mul'chenko state that it is not the inferiority of Soviet scientific personnel or equipment which is mainly responsible for the generally low level of citations made to Soviet work by foreign scientists, but ineffective communication. According to them: 'It is quite obviously to do with this, in our country the provision of scientific information is badly organised. The delay in the movement of new ideas along communication channels is intolerably great'.[21]

Nalimov and Mul'chenko say that new ideas are delayed as a result of the difficulty of receiving foreign journals punctually and also by the slow publication of articles written by Soviet scientists in Soviet journals. They claim that advances made by Soviet scientists are devalued by their late appearance in print, with the result that only the most significant ones succeed in making an international impact.[22]

Obstructions and delays in these formal communication channels are regarded as having especially serious consequences for Soviet scientists because, unlike their Western counterparts, they cannot easily take part in the informal international communication networks which grow up among scientists of different countries who are engaged on similar lines of research. This is illustrated by studies of international networks of informally communicating scientists which show Soviet participation to be, at best, marginal.[23] Additionally, opportunities for initiating and developing such links remain very limited, in spite of some recent improvements. Academic exchanges between the Soviet Union and Western countries involve only a tiny fraction of their respective scientific communities,[24] whilst a significant proportion of Soviet scientists regularly fails to appear at the international conferences and seminars where their attendance has been anticipated.[25]

As a result, Soviet scientists are more likely to have to depend for foreign information on the appearance of published papers in foreign journals, the contents of which may be already widely known abroad through the informal contacts that exist among foreign researchers.[26] Deprived of direct means of communication, Soviet scientists are more likely to experience the publication of new results as a fait accompli. Nalimov and Mul'chenko have estimated that this isolation may result in a lag of at least a year between the work of Soviet scientists and their opposite numbers abroad.[27]

The significance, both intellectual and social, of the marginal position occupied by Soviet scientists, in the context of the world scientific system, may be more fully appreciated in the light of Derek de Solla Price's analysis of the structure of citations described earlier in this chapter. Given the interrelated mode of citations, which Price identifies as characteristic of the natural sciences, the relatively low level of citation made to the work of Soviet scientists by non-Soviet scientists may be interpreted to mean that a disproportionately large number of Soviet scientific papers are not well integrated into the pattern of recent and highly interconnected papers, which constitute what Price calls the 'research front' of each discipline.

The links that exist between papers in the form of citations signify social as well as cognitive relationships. Citations are the most impersonal connection in research networks or invisible colleges. Participation in a research network is significant for scientists not only because it enables them to keep abreast of the latest developments in the field, in advance of publication, but also because of the important role played by these informal groups in the process of research itself. This role is described by Michael Mulkay in the following way:

> Research networks are the social units responsible for scientific innovation in the sense that their members encourage or discourage certain lines of work, in the sense that the initial response to research findings is made by a particular network, and in the sense that approved results are taken up and disseminated by the network's members.[28]

Research networks are, therefore, more than a means of keeping scientists informed, important though this is. They also direct the course of research by acting as the mechanism which reflects the degree of recognition forthcoming from the researchers in the field for contributions made by any one of their number. It is in this sense that the significance of citations as the most routine means of recording recognition may be more fully understood.

It is the realisation that the social and intellectual processes of science are interlinked in the roles performed by research networks which makes the analysis of citations by Nalimov and Mul'chenko so informative and, in the Soviet context, so provocative and unusual. Their work is interesting not only because they demonstrate that Soviet scientists would be better informed if they were permitted freer contact with their colleagues abroad, but because they also ask how adequately science in the USSR can be managed if the influence of international research networks is not allowed to be more directly felt in Soviet research establishments.[29]

It may be concluded that an important distinguishing feature of the working environment of Soviet scientists is the degree to which it is insulated from the direct influence of foreign scientists and, in particular, from the international scientific networks which grow up among them. This does not mean that Soviet scientists lack informal professional relationships altogether, but that the groups into which they form themselves are, in general, bereft of developed international links characteristic of the natural sciences as practised outside the USSR. It is to these domestic scientific groups that attention is now turned.

Of great help in clarifying the character of informal relations among Soviet scientists is an observation made by Thane Gustafson. He points out that, whereas in the United States scientists working in any one specialist area are likely to be dispersed among numerous university faculties, in the Soviet Union they are just as likely to be concentrated in a large specialised research institute. 'For the individual researcher', he notes, 'a large part of his invisible college is not invisible at all but working in the same building.'[30] So, from the point of view of the Soviet natural scientist, the more energetic forms of personal communication may appear to be dispensable. An American scientist may find that he or she lacks a research community altogether if he or she fails to pick up the telephone, write letters and frequently attend distant seminars and conferences, but a Soviet counterpart may be able to exist quite comfortably by crossing the corridor or walking from one building to the next.

Differences in the working situation of Soviet and North American scientists can, of course, be overdrawn. Quite clearly, the environment in which a scientist operates will be affected by the specific demands of the discipline. The degree of dependence on sophisticated equipment, for example, will impose certain uniformities independently of the actual place where research is carried out. Scientists requiring large experimental facilities, like accelerators, are more likely to be concentrated in specialist teams than those involved in more theoretical disciplines, whether they are working in California or Siberia.[31] Alternatively, someone working in a highly specialised, sparsely populated field may be obliged to maintain contacts with people spread all over the world in order to participate in the exchange of ideas and information at all. As suggested by Zhores Medvedev's account of his experiences in researching in the area of gerontology, Soviet scientists in these kinds of specialised areas may find themselves in a particularly invidious position.[32]

As far as the internal arrangements of Soviet research institutes are concerned, one of the most useful sources of information is a study of the Institute of Molecular Biology of the USSR Academy of Sciences.[33] Informal interlaboratory relations were traced from the time when the Institute was established in 1959 through until 1977. During this period informal relations were observed to grow and assume more complex forms. This was associated with an increase in the number of interdisciplinary units and the overall expansion of the Institute with the opening of many new laboratories.

It was observed that the informal arrangements tended to outgrow the formal framework. This occurred with the burgeoning of personal communications between the members of thematic groups, into which laboratories are subdivided, which could be observed for a year or two prior to the transformation of these groups into independent, officially recognised units. An analogous process whereby successful personal exploratory themes were adopted as components of the Institute's plan over a similar period was also evident. The formal structure and the official goals of the Institute could thus be seen to respond to the changing informal relations of scientists. The authors of the study also claim that the informal relations they observed were developing not merely in response to domestic stimuli, but to 'a new stage in the development of the problems of molecular biology on the world scale'.[34]

It could be that the Institute of Molecular Biology is atypical among the research establishments of the USSR Academy of Sciences. In the first place this discipline needed to be almost completely reconstructed after the damaging effects of Lysenkoism; indeed, the authors note that the Institute was established 'practically in an empty space'.[35] The combination of relative newness, probably youthful staff, and the priority allocated to this field during the past decade may have acted to bring about a more flexible structure than in some of the more traditional establishments. However, there are a number of institutes in the USSR Academy of Sciences in which one might also expect to find a good fit between the patterns of informal working relations and the formal structure of the institutes themselves. Such complementary arrangements could make for greater degrees of cohesion among the members of specialist groups in the USSR than in the dispersed inter-national groups more characteristic of scientists outside the Soviet Union.

Looking beyond the individual institute, it is apparent that Soviet scientists not only are brought together in large specialised research establishments but they are also concentrated, perhaps to a unique degree, in the major cities and 'science towns'. With upwards of a quarter of a million scientific workers among its population, Moscow possesses a large scientific community within the city limits.[36] In addition to the concentration of leading specialists in the same research establishments, the tendency for research institutes to be clustered in the main cities and other scientific centres has provided conditions which are conducive to the formation of working relation-ships between, as well as within, research establishments. Develop-ments in science can rarely be contained within a rigid institutional framework for long and there are no special reasons to suppose that the Soviet scientific system is exempt. That this indeed seems to be the case is supported by the findings of a number of Soviet studies of the social organisation of science.

For example, a study of the effect of periodically organised conferences on the growth of informal links among Soviet scientists investigating the origin of life shows how successive meetings encouraged the formation of an extensive multi-disciplinary invisible college.[37] Another piece of research has demonstrated that, under certain circumstances, ties between scientists working in different research establishments may become stronger than those existing between scientists working in the same one. It also showed that such ties were greatly valued by scientists who sought to perpetuate them.[38]

After analysing a number of studies carried out by Soviet scholars bearing on these kinds of issues, Linda Lubrano summarises their findings in two main conclusions: first, that Soviet scientists tend to behave in accordance with their professional interests, in spite of formal institutional arrangements, and second, that informal professional interaction is a natural part of scientific work in the USSR. She concludes that: 'The self-generation of scientific communities and the operation of professional norms are similar, in this respect, to the behaviour of scientists in other countries'.[39]

From the foregoing it can be seen that there are good reasons for believing that Soviet natural scientists organise themselves in ways which are broadly similar to those of scientists elsewhere in the world, with the proviso that the informal networks which grow up in the Soviet Union only marginally interact with those that develop abroad. Formal communication between Soviet scientists and their foreign counterparts through the pages of professional journals does not, in general, appear to form part of more extensive or sustained international networks of direct professional relationships of the kind which are commonly found among scientists outside the USSR.

The quality of equipment and personnel

Nalimov and Mul'chenko reject the interpretation which states that citation data reflects the inferiority of Soviet work when judged in terms of internationally accepted standards. Instead, they argue that obstructions in channels of communications between Soviet and foreign scientists delay the Soviet research effort and reduce the impact made by its published results when they eventually appear.

The contention that the low citation of Soviet work is a consequence of lateness rather than a reflection of its intrinsic merits has been questioned by Ronald Amann in the context of his study of research and development in the Soviet chemical industry. He suggests that Nalimov and Mul'chenko fail to pursue their own line of reasoning to its logical conclusion, noting that: 'Poor information flows may, to some extent, reduce the level of citation, but they will also retard the *level* of scientific development itself.'[40] Only in those cases where slow publication by Soviet journals could be demonstrated to have allowed Western scientists to beat their Soviet counterparts into print would lateness not also mean inferiority. Although a number of Soviet journals still take inordinately long periods to publish articles submitted to them, and although the quality of Soviet scientific editing has often been criticised, it would seem improbable that these kinds of problems alone could explain the generally low levels of citation attracted by Soviet published papers.[41]

If one accepts Amann's suggestion that Soviet research is weak as well as late, then this immediately raises the question of whether Nalimov and Mul'chenko over-emphasise communication barriers in explaining the low levels of citation to Soviet work. Indeed Amann argues that the position of Soviet scientists in this respect may not be as invidious as the Soviet authors make out. On the 'input' side it is by no means certain that the provision of information through the reference journals published by the Soviet scientific and technical information services is drastically inferior to arrangements found in Western countries. On the 'output' side it is suggested that the detailed classification systems of reference journals, together with the availability of articles in translation, facilitates the identification of significant Soviet research, thus reducing the impact of the language barrier.[42]

In support of these arguments Amann is able to show that some of Nalimov and Mul'chenko's data may be interpreted in ways which give rise to conclusions somewhat different from their own. For example, they show that in spite of the generally low level of citation attracted by Soviet work abroad, articles of certain Soviet scientists none the less attract considerable amounts of citation from Western counterparts. This, says Amann, may indicate that obstructions in communication channels are insufficiently serious to prevent the identification by foreign scientists of significant Soviet research when it appears. Equally articles in one of the journals studied by the Soviet authors did not attract higher levels of citation than the others, although the journal was available in translation.[43] Again this may be taken to suggest that the impact of communication barriers may have been overstated by Nalimov and Mul'chenko.

Amann's arguments may be countered on the grounds that too much emphasis is placed on the formal channels of communication via the pages of scientific journals, leading to the underestimation of the significance of barriers which prevent the development of direct working relationships between Soviet scientists and their opposite numbers abroad. One of the most enlightening aspects of Nalimov and Mul'chenko's work is their description of the roles played by invisible colleges in the circulation of information prior to publication and in the identification of research priorities and the evaluation of results. Whilst one might argue that Amann pays insufficient attention to these important aspects of their work, there can be little doubt that his point, that barriers to formal communication cannot on their own account for the low level of citation of Soviet work abroad, is persuasive.

This conclusion is not only based on the reasons advanced by Amann but arises from the consideration of other factors which also appear to influence the effectiveness of the Soviet research effort significantly. There is, for example, a good deal of evidence which suggests that a lack of sophisticated equipment and adequate supplies of materials needed in laboratories impedes the development of science in the USSR. Again, some of Nalimov and Mul'chenko's data lends itself to this interpretation just as it does to the communication barriers explanation they prefer, for they show that those sub-fields of analytical chemistry which are most dependent upon sophisticated equipment attracted lower rates of citation abroad than those which relied to a lesser extent on advanced technologies.[44] Whilst there are a number of well-known cases where the shortcomings of the Soviet scientific instruments industry have held back Soviet research,[45] it has recently been suggested that the dramatic advances now taking place in instrumentation, especially as a result of the rapid development of microelectronics, may be comprehensively reducing the effectiveness of Soviet research. Thane Gustafson, for example, believes that the difficulties involved in providing instrumentation and supplies needed by Soviet research establishments are the most important single cause of the relatively disappointing performance of the USSR in many areas of the natural sciences.[46]

In addition to the problems arising from poor international communications and inadequate supplies of equipment and materials, there is the question of the quality of Soviet natural scientists themselves. As pointed out in the previous chapters, the academies of sciences constitute the elite of the Soviet research system, and competition to enter the universities and the more academically orientated higher educational institutions is intense. Whereas this facilitates the concentration of talent in the natural sciences there are a number of reasons why this may not always be translated into effective research.

The first of these concerns the divorce between teaching and research characteristic of the Soviet higher educational system. Whilst this problem seems to have been overcome by a number of prestigious institutions, notably Leningrad Polytechnical Institute, Moscow's Physico-Technical and Engineering-Physics Institutes and Novosibirsk University, the recognised need to extend this kind of research training to other disciplines, besides physics, suggests that the traditional division between teaching and research still negatively affects the quality of Soviet scientists. As a result, talented young people may experience a lag in acquiring the habits of independence required for research and fail to achieve their potential as rapidly as might otherwise have been the case.[47]

The second reason is associated with the pressures on Soviet natural scientists to undertake work of an applied character. In addition to the responsibility to demonstrate the technical potential of fundamental research, the academies of sciences also act as technical trouble-shooters stepping in to solve some of the problems encountered by applied research institutes in developing new products and processes for industry. The superior quality of the scientists employed in the academies of sciences thus brings with it the pressure to render ad hoc assistance to industrial research establishments, which involves work unlikely to contribute to the scientific reputations of those required to undertake it.

Finally there is the role of political criteria in the selection and advancement of scientists. Today natural scientists no longer have to worry about the ideological acceptability of their disciplines, which are all now officially considered to be uniquely compatible with Marxism-Leninism. Soviet scientists are, however, still encouraged to make a political contribution by illustrating this purported relationship with examples of successful Soviet research and cannot altogether retreat into agnosticism without jeopardising their chances of promotion. Thus non-professional criteria remain relevant in assessing the performance of the Soviet scientist. In addition to imposing the burden of carrying out social obligations, as party-inspired work is designated, the use of extra-professional criteria may result in contentious promotions and, in extreme cases, to the advancement of scientists to positions of responsibility beyond their competence. So whilst there are no grounds for believing that Soviet natural scientists are somehow inherently inferior to their foreign counterparts, there are grounds for believing that the character of their training and certain aspects of their working conditions may impede their development and reduce their effectiveness.

CONCLUSION

It may be concluded that, by analysing the factors which combine to explain the weaknesses of the Soviet research performance, the nature of the working environment of the Soviet scientist is also clarified. Whilst it is difficult to decide whether it is problems associated with the provision of information, of equipment or of personnel which exert the greatest influence on the quality of Soviet research, the choice is clearer when trying to understand the social relations of Soviet natural scientists.

The reason for this is that the processes whereby information is transmitted in science are inextricably linked with those concerned in the evaluation of the research and the assignment of professional recognition. The isolation of Soviet scientists from international scientific communities thus affects the Soviet research environment fundamentally.

In the first place, isolation prevents Soviet scientists from working in an environment which consists of all those conducting research in their respective fields. Consequently key potential colleagues will always be out of reach. In the second place, isolation reduces the size of the immediate audience of scientists competent to judge the work of Soviet researchers. This blunts the impact of Soviet research because it is likely to appear unannounced, unanticipated and thus be more open to misinterpretation. Here it is important to appreciate that the conventions governing the presentation of results differ between Soviet and Western journals and this has been known to obscure the immediate significance of Soviet work when submitted to Western scientific journals.[48] The inability to maintain direct contact with the international audience of fellow researchers not only reduces the probability of 'applause', in the form of recognition, but also weakens its impact on the Soviet scientist should it be forthcoming. The full force of international recognition, therefore, cannot be readily transmitted to the Soviet scientists which means that one of the most important motives for undertaking original research is blunted in their case.

Soviet isolation therefore reduces the influence of informal networks in the research process, weakens their authority in the research institute and lessens their impact on the management of science. As a result the hierarchies of Soviet scientific institutions are more open to influences arising outside science in the setting of research priorities and in the conduct and evaluation of research.

5 Planning and Leadership in the Soviet Scientific System

The previous chapter dealt with informal groups which grow up among natural scientists. Although these groups play a crucial role in the generation of scientific knowledge, it is through the formal institutions of the academies of sciences that plans are formulated, tasks assigned and resources allocated. The question which this chapter addresses concerns the degree to which the informal relationships of science can be accommodated by the Soviet Union's system of centralised institutions, plans and leadership.

INSTITUTIONS: THE HYBRID CHARACTER OF THE USSR ACADEMY OF SCIENCES

The statute of the USSR Academy of Sciences identifies two principal responsibilities. In the first place, it designates the Academy as the nation's leading scientific establishment embracing the most celebrated Soviet scholars and scientists. In the second place, the Academy is identified as an agency of the Soviet state responsible to the USSR Council of Ministers for the administration of research in its own establishments, and for the supervision of research in the natural and social sciences wherever else it is undertaken.[1]

The USSR Academy of Sciences is, therefore, something of a hybrid of the worlds of scholarship and administration. As such it has some unusual features when compared with other organs of the Soviet state. For example, the Academy's most important policy-making bodies, surmounted by the Praesidium, are elected by and to some extent answerable to the General Meeting of full and corresponding members, which the statute recognises as the Academy's highest body. A similar relationship obtains between the general meetings of the 17 divisions into which the USSR Academy is organised, and the divisional bureaux through which day-to-day administrative leadership of science is effected.

Over and above this many scientists are drawn into the Academy's decision-making processes as members of commissions attached to the Praesidium or the divisions. Most of these commissions exist to monitor the progress of different disciplines and subject areas, with a view to providing an informed framework within which science may be planned.[2] So whilst the Soviet fundamental research effort is concentrated to a degree which is unique among leading industrial nations, the associated tendency towards centralisation is ameliorated by the predominance of scientists in the decision-making agencies of the USSR Academy of Sciences and the unusual responsiveness of these agencies when compared with those found in other areas of state administration.

The hybrid character of the USSR Academy of Sciences extends beyond its central machinery and reaches down through the hierarchies of the research institutes themselves. Important administrative responsibilities concerning the planning and provisioning of research are carried by the director of a research institute, the deputies, and the departmental and laboratory chiefs, all of whom sit on the academic council through which an institute's affairs are managed.[3] Below them, the rank-and-file junior and senior researchers may be assigned responsibility for some part of the planned work, but these posts are not designated as carrying administrative responsibility; the latter usually denotes positions giving control over people as well as over research.[4]

The interlinking of scientific and administrative responsibilities is a consequence both of the concentration of the Soviet fundamental research effort in specialist institutes and of the unitary hierarchy which presides over them in the form of the USSR Academy of Sciences. In the English-speaking world, where much fundamental research is carried out by the members of university departments organised on a disciplinary basis, invisible colleges do not usually coincide with institutional boundaries. In these circumstances, the scientist's professional authority is usually defined, to a considerable extent, by relations which extend beyond the hierarchy of the employing institution. In the Soviet Union the concentration of researchers in one or a few establishments, and the consequent overlap between informal research networks and the hierarchies of research institutions, means that administrative authority can more easily play a direct part in determining the recognition which a scientist's work receives even if this does not correspond with informal professional opinion. This makes it particularly significant to assess the extent to which a coincidence is achieved between scientific standing and hierarchical position.

PLANNING: THE PRESSURES OF TECHNOLOGY AND BUREAUCRACY

A distinctive feature of the working environment of the Soviet scientist is the system of centralised state planning. The majority of the research undertaken in the institutes of the USSR Academy of Sciences is subject to plans approved and co-ordinated by its central machinery and by other agencies of the Soviet state responsible for various aspects of science policy.[5] In the Soviet context, therefore, an additional set of criteria, in the shape of the plans, operates between the scientist and the professional recognition generated by a person's work among fellow specialists in the field. In contrast to the invisible college, in which a scientist's contribution is judged by professional equals, plan fulfilment introduces a hierarchical dimension into the research relationship. The degree to which the professional criterion of scientific recognition coheres with the administrative criterion of plan fulfilment can, therefore, be expected to affect the significance of research and the efficiency with which it is carried out.

There are at least two important factors which affect the impact of planning on the research undertaken by Academy scientists. The first is the way in which plans are compiled and the second is the way in which they are executed. The way in which plans are compiled and acted upon differs according to whether their objectives are principally exploratory, that is involving a substantial commitment to the generation of new knowledge, or technical, that is primarily aimed at developing a new product or process.

In the case of the former, the influence of scientists in the compilation of plans, and the flexibility with which they are interpreted, appears to be much greater than in the case of the latter. The five-year plans for research in the natural and social sciences have, by and large, been regarded as the exclusive responsibility of the USSR Academy of Sciences. They are compiled on the basis of existing research commitments and proposals arising from within the institutes, which are duly considered and co-ordinated by their directors, before progressing to the appropriate divisions of the

Academy en route to becoming part of the draft five-year plan, eventually presented to the Praesidium of the USSR Academy of Sciences. Although other state bodies concerned with the formulation of science policy, such as the USSR State Committee for Science and Technology, may be consulted, the draft plan has always been very much the Academy's own creation and recognised as its own affair.[6]

The plans for fundamental research are also distinguished by the manner in which they are interpreted and acted upon. Traditionally they have been interpreted with an unusual and possibly unique degree of flexibility, being considered as guides rather than as rigid programmes. As Academician V. A. Kirillin, a former deputy chairman of the USSR Council of Ministers and one-time Chairman of the State Committee for Science and Technology, observed:

Planning the development of fundamental research as part of the state plan has a more recommendatory than obligatory character. Considering that it is practically impossible to foresee exactly where and in what areas of fundamental research an important new discovery or decisive advance may be made, it is scarcely expedient to give concrete expression to the state plan in that part concerned with the development of fundamental research.[7]

Whilst scientists may experience a good deal of autonomy in the formulation and interpretation of plans in fundamental research, their responsibilities do not end here, for both the USSR and the republican academies of sciences carry out a considerable amount of technical work. For example, about 650 out of 1450 research problems undertaken by the USSR Academy of Sciences during the ninth five-year plan, which was concluded in 1975, were of a technical type.[8] The government's concern to encourage technically useful work also appears to have been influencing the method of planning fundamental research. Since the early seventies the 'Integrated Programme of Scientific and Technical Progress and its Social Consequences' has emerged as the main framework for planning all scientific and technical research. The 'Integrated Programme' specifies the principal solvable scientific and technical problems thought to hold out greatest promise for both the advancement of science in the USSR and the development of the Soviet economy in general in the period 1976–90.[9] During the tenth five-year plan, concluded at the end of 1980, the bulk of appropriations for science were reported to have been intended for such projects.[10] Although scientists and scholars of the USSR Academy of Sciences played the major role in the preparation of this programme it cannot be regarded as the Academy's exclusive affair, for it is considered an essential guide to the directions in which the Soviet economy may develop in the medium and long term.

Associated with this programme is the introduction of a more rigorous system of planning in the USSR Academy of Sciences itself, known as 'special-purpose planning'. Currently this is being energetically put forward by the planning and financial organs attached to the Praesidium of the USSR Academy of Sciences, with a view to tying institutes to detailed research proposals more amenable to external checks. Although still at the experimental stage, this style of planning is seen by its advocates as a replacement for the more permissive approach characterised by the observations of Kirillin, quoted above.[11]

In addition to their planned involvement in technical projects of national importance, institutes of the USSR and republican academies may also enter into contracts to carry out work for industrial enterprises or other external bodies. Contractual commitments expanded so rapidly in some research institutes in the early 1970s that some anxiety was publicly expressed about the academies being deflected from their proper tasks.[12] In addition to this kind of work, institutes of the academies of sciences act as industrial consultants. Some idea of the scale of these extra tasks is suggested by the example of the Institute of Chemical Physics of the USSR Academy of Sciences which is reported to have been carrying out 6000 consultancies a year.[13]

The extent of the academies' involvement in technical projects influences the style of management as well as the content of research. In undertaking technical work scientists are ultimately responding to the requirements of their customers rather than the priorities of science. As a result, technical projects are usually more rigidly planned and administered than those of a more exploratory character. Here it is interesting to note that scientists are said to have expressed reservations about the stricter planning of the special-purpose type currently being introduced into the institutes of the USSR Academy of Sciences. One reason for this is that it requires them, in the interests of developing long-term technical programmes, to reveal details of their research before it has reached fruition, thereby jeopardising their chances of claiming priority once the results are published. This is one way in which the demands of planning and the achievement of academic recognition can, under certain circumstances, conflict.[14]

The system of state planning as a whole also exerts an impact on the conduct of research independently of the flexibility with which different plans are compiled and acted upon. The activities of drawing up plans, checking and reporting on their progress, and trying to ensure that the resources are there to carry them out, take up a good deal of scientists' time and often force them to cope with unforeseen difficulties.

Some idea of the impact of these responsibilities may be gained from surveys designed to investigate how scientists allocate their time between the different tasks which compose their working day. The time budgets, based on these investigations, generally make a distinction between organisational and research work. Although the content of these and other categories of work is not always specified in detail, when this does occur organisational work is defined as being primarily concerned with the planning and supplying of research. Analyses of the scientist's working day show that organisational work takes up a significant proportion of it. They also show that this proportion increases substantially with seniority and that such tasks generally take up more time in experimental than theoretical research establishments.

For example, in a number of research institutions studied in the USSR and Ukrainian Academies of Sciences it was found that scientists occupying the more senior posts in experimental research spent between 30 and 60 per cent of their working time in the institute on organisational work, whereas scientists in similar positions engaged in theoretical research spent between 20 and 50 per cent of their time on such tasks.[15] Similar findings have been reported from the research establishments of the Kazakh Academy of Sciences, where those in responsible posts were observed to be spending over 40 per cent of their working time on organisational activities.[16] It appears that scientists occupying the more senior positions, which give them greatest influence over the direction taken by research and the best chance of achieving a good fit between their personal interests and their research plans, are, paradoxically, likely to find themselves spending less and less time actually carrying out research. Whilst this may not necessarily result in losing touch with the newest developments in the field, or with the personal interests and capabilities of

subordinates, the risk is always there, even for competent and con-
scientious researchers, as the following observation makes abundantly
clear.

> The able and energetic physicist, by now several years on after
> beginning scientific work, is pushed up the rungs of the organ-
> isational ladder and, as a rule, becomes the leader of a separate
> group or laboratory. With this the volume of purely organisational
> work rapidly grows, which breaks down into many petty operations
> of an administrative character necessary to ensure normal
> conditions for the conduct of research. With every year the
> proportion of time taken up with such functions increases and the
> opportunity for direct participation in experimental work is more
> and more restricted. Thus can occur the 'self-exclusion of the
> experimental physicist from experimentation'.[17]

One of the biggest headaches for the directors of scientific
institutions, and especially for those involved in experimental research
requiring specialised materials and sophisticated equipment, is
ensuring an adequate supply of the things they need to carry out their
work. Whilst scientists are peculiarly sensitive to blockages in
information channels, they share a common problem with managers
throughout the Soviet economy with respect to the unreliable
material-technical supply system (*mattekhsnab*).[18] This affects
research establishments by taking up the time of senior staff in seeking
ways of coping with the absence or inadequacy of supplies and by
forcing changes and adjustments in research schedules. It is not
surprising, therefore, that junior staff have registered dissatisfaction
with their conditions as their work frequently consists of the
routine manufacture of reagents or other substances necessary for the
experiments they were actually trained to perform, or that senior
scientists find it hard to spend time in the laboratories when they are
searching for ways of securing equipment needed to operate them
properly.[19] Thus apparently arbitrary instructions, when viewed from
below, may sometimes be the consequence of a time-consuming and
inefficient system of national planning rather than an authentic
expression of the style of leadership preferred by senior scientists.

LEADERSHIP: THE ADVANTAGES OF FLEXIBILITY

The directors of research establishments are subject to many cross-pressures as they occupy a position at the interface between the planning system and the rank-and-file scientists. The way they respond to these pressures may be expected to exert a significant influence on the morale and efficiency of the scientists for whom they are responsible. In consequence, Soviet scientific research institutions have been shown to accommodate a variety of styles of leadership. Some idea of the different approaches which have grown up may be gained from a study which arranges them along a spectrum from the most to the least authoritarian.[20] The styles range from what is referred to as 'pure *edinonachalie*' to 'parliamentary'. The term *edinonachalie* literally means 'one-man management', but it also connotes the tough bosses with quasi-political powers prominent in Soviet industry during the pre-war five-year plans. In the context of a scientific research institute today, it signifies an autocratic style of leadership where rank-and-file scientists are permitted no say in the formulation, distribution or choice of methods appropriate to the tasks undertaken, which are split up so that no one scientist is responsible for a complete project. Moving away from this extreme, a more moderate style of 'one-man management' is described where scientists are given complete tasks to carry out and allowed to develop their own methods, but permitted no voice in the formulation of research projects, which remains the prerogative of the director.

The third and fourth styles are identified as 'consultative' and 'parliamentary'. The 'consultative' style relies on inducing, rather than instructing, scientists to carry out tasks and seeks to avoid undue interference in their work. The 'parliamentary' style depicts a situation where the members of an institute's academic council share in decision-making and rank-and-file scientists participate in the formulation of research proposals and choose their own methods of research. In these circumstances leaders are distinguished from their colleagues only in so far as it is they who take final responsibility for decisions arrived at collectively.

There is a variety of evidence which relates more or less directly to the styles of leadership found in the academies of sciences. A survey of 1500 academy scientific workers, predominantly drawn from research establishments in the natural sciences, revealed that the vast majority of those sampled, some 77 per cent, were generally satisfied with their leaders and that 67 per cent were similarly content with the extent to which they were consulted by them.[21] Levels of job satisfaction were also investigated, by examining the degree of correspondence which existed between the personal interests of the scientists and the topics on which they were required to work. Although the vast majority of scientists claimed that their research topic fully or basically coincided with their scientific interests, lower levels of satisfaction were registered by junior scientists and by those exclusively engaged on projects of an applied type.[22]

Whilst common sense suggests that higher levels of job satisfaction might be expected to be associated with consultative styles of leadership, this cannot be demonstrated solely on the basis of the data assembled here, even though most scientists were shown to be satisfied with the degree to which their leaders took account of their opinions. It should be borne in mind that there is a strong authoritarian tradition in the Soviet higher educational system which might mean that Soviet scientists, particularly the younger ones, may be satisfied with less consultation than their Western counterparts.[23] There is, however, circumstantial evidence which suggests that flexible styles of leadership are preferred by Soviet scientists. When complaints about leaders have been investigated these have generally criticised authoritarianism rather than permissiveness. For example, studies carried out in the Leningrad and Irkutsk institutes of the USSR Academy of Sciences both identified rude and bureaucratic behaviour on the part of leaders as arousing the resentment of scientists and precipitating conflicts among them.[24]

If the prevailing preferences of scientists for different types of leaders cannot be conclusively established, firmer evidence exists which shows that consultative styles of leadership are associated with high-quality research. On the basis of a study of a number of scientific collectives carried out in several natural science institutes of the USSR Academy of Sciences, it was concluded:

> In the [decentralised] groups, greater democracy exists in the taking of decisions concerning the selection of cadres and in the distribution of effort, etc. Among ten USSR Academy of Sciences institutes observed by us, collectives of the second [decentralised] type constituted the majority in the most authoritative of them. The level of training and the level of qualification of the rank-and-file scientists are comparatively high and the leaders' relations with them are more collegial than of a boss–subordinate type.[25]

It was also noted that authoritative scientists were more prevalent among the leaders of the subdivisions of decentralised collectives and that these exhibited a number of other strengths. For example, in decentralised collectives rank-and-file researchers were found to appreciate more fully the long-term significance of the problems they were investigating and tended to form more satisfactory informal relationships with their colleagues.[26]

The flexibility of arrangements within institutes has also been positively linked with the effectiveness of research by studies which have focussed on the opportunities open to scientists to change from one specialism to another in the course of their careers. For example, less than a third of 1400 scientists sampled in surveys carried out in Leningrad and Riga were found to be involved in research topics which fully corresponded with their higher educational specialisms. Whilst this may not always be a positive indication, since movement can occur for all kinds of reasons, it was found in this instance that over half of those who had moved from their original fields were working in newly developing areas, corresponding more closely to their personal scientific interests.[27]

Involvement in newly developing fields has been shown to be of crucial importance. It has been found to be associated with positive attitudes to research, co-operative relations with colleagues and higher levels of qualification. Accordingly scientists in newly emerging areas were observed to work harder and more productively, putting in extra hours and publishing more frequently than scientists unable to find such congenial work.[28]

The importance of institutional flexibility has also been demonstrated by evidence which shows that transferring to new fields is not correlated with frequent changes of employment. On the contrary, higher rates of professional mobility seem to support more stable institutions. Flexible internal arrangements apparently encourage researchers involved in emerging fields to associate the successful completion of a project with reward or advancement within the same establishment. Leaving the institute is more likely to be precipitated by dissatisfaction with working conditions or some other negative experience.[29] This is also supported by studies which have disclosed high rates of labour turnover in branch research institutes rigidly tied to the requirements of specific industries.[30]

It may be concluded that if institutional arrangements are flexible enough to accommodate informal relations and a genuine correspondence is achieved between scientific and administrative authority, then an institute's leadership is less likely to rely on authoritarian means of management, as many administrative functions will be performed informally by scientists in the ordinary course of their research. Professional recognition is the motive-force rather than instructions from above, and new directions of research will be generated and assessed as part of the normal process of intellectual exchange.

When formal arrangements are inflexible and institutional and scientific authority diverge, informal networks either may fail to develop or, if they do, their presence may lead to conflict between the genuine and official leadership in the research establishment. Lacking the capacity to tap the self-managing potential of informal networks, the leadership is more likely to be forced to rely on administrative authority when formulating and distributing tasks and motivating scientists.

CONCLUSION

The style of leadership occupies a pivotal role in determining the degree of compatibility which exists between the informal professional requirements of natural scientists and the plans and internal arrangements of the establishments which employ them. The research carried out by Soviet social scientists supports the proposition that flexible institutional arrangements and responsive, democratic styles of leadership are more likely to occur in prestigious establishments led by authoritative scientists capable of encouraging talent without fearing for their own status.

What also emerges is considerable support for the opinion, expressed many years ago by Kapitsa, that Soviet research establishments suffer if they are led by scientists who cannot combine scientific talent with organising skills.[31] The importance of combining these attributes clearly arises from the fusion of scientific and administrative roles in Soviet academic hierarchies, and from the demands that the Soviet planning system places on those occupying responsible positions in all institutions which depend on scarce resources and skilled manpower to achieve their goals. Being a good director continues to involve achieving a fine balance by presenting proposals which are concrete enough to attract resources, yet sufficiently open-ended to permit a reasonable degree of freedom in the management of research.

Writing in the early 1960s, Kapitsa considered that an unacceptable degree of divergence had arisen between the administrative and scientific qualifications of those occupying senior posts in Soviet research institutions. He observed:

It is very difficult at present to attract able scientists into responsible posts as heads of laboratories and directors of institutes. With us these posts are frequently filled by people with administrative skills, but without creative scientific qualifications, and as a result of this collectives are beginning to work badly.[32]

Subsequent assessments have generally been more favourable, stressing that, by and large, leading positions in the natural sciences are filled by competent scientists of some standing in their particular fields who have gained the respect of their colleagues.[33] Today the opinion is widespread among Soviet natural scientists that the efficiency of research would be enhanced if the rights of institute directors were to be strengthened with respect to the recruitment and dismissal of staff and the management of the research and pay funds.[34] This suggests that many of the problems encountered in the running of research establishments are seen by scientists as arising from sources external to the institutes themselves and would be eliminated if greater autonomy were granted to the directors of research establishments. If such a step were to be taken, it would reduce the persisting discrepancy between the decentralised arrangements of informal research communities and the centralised framework of state institutions with which they co-exist.

6 Natural Scientists and the Communist Party: Structure, Functions and Membership

The USSR Academy of Sciences carries the principal responsibility for formulating and executing policy in fundamental research. Here, as in all other areas of state responsibility, such activities are supervised by the Communist Party which exerts, thereby, a profound influence on the working environment of Soviet scientists. It is the nature of this influence and the broader question of the character of the relationship existing between the Communist Party and the Soviet scientific community that the remaining chapters seek to clarify.

This chapter provides three of the basic ingredients necessary for the examination of these issues. In the first place it describes how the Communist Party is organised with respect to scientific institutions, in the second place it outlines the main kinds of function carried out by the party in science, and finally it assembles the available information about party membership among scientists and discusses some of the problems of interpretation which arise.

COMMUNIST PARTY ORGANISATION AND NATURAL SCIENTISTS

The basic unit of the Communist Party is the primary organisation. At the beginning of 1981 there were over 414 000 such organisations, located almost entirely in the place of work.[1] Greater variation in size and organisation is found at this, the lowest, level of the party hierarchy than at any other. A minimum of three members is sufficient to form a party organisation, while at the other extreme the primary organisations of large establishments may contain several thousand people.[2] Moscow University's party organisation, for example, contains more than 7000 members divided up into numerous groups, each one as large as the primary organisations of many smaller establishments.[3] Such large organisations are the exception; more than 80 per cent of the Soviet Communist Party's primary organisations have less than 50 members and fewer than 7 per cent more than 100.[4]

The responsibilities and internal arrangements of primary organisations differ according to size. Large organisations with over 300 members are entitled to elect a committee, whilst smaller ones elect a bureau. Those with 150 members or more may have a full-time secretary. Very large primary organisations like Moscow University's possess some of the rights normally exercised by party organisations at the immediately superior district level. These rights usually concern the confirmation of new members.[5]

The organisation of the Communist Party above the primary level may be best introduced by describing the procedures for selecting those who compose the local, regional and national committees and their associated bureaux and secretariats. The process begins with the primary organisations which elect delegates to attend the city or district conferences that are convened every other year. At these conferences new district or city committees are elected along with the delegates who will attend the next tier of party conferences at the regional level. This is repeated until delegates have been selected to attend the national Party Congress which meets in Moscow every five years.[6]

The bureaux and committees set up at each level of the party hierarchy are not exclusively composed of party functionaries but embody national or local elites drawn from a variety of state and public organisations. At the national level the Politburo always contains the Chairman of the USSR Council of Ministers together with some of those in charge of the more important ministries and state committees, which have included Foreign Affairs, Defence and the KGB, along with top party leaders. Of those elected to the current Central Committee only some 40 per cent are full-time party officials, the remaining 60 per cent being mostly drawn from among those who occupy senior positions in the ministerial hierarchies, the military, and the trade unions and other public organisations.[7] In recent decades the Presidency of the USSR Academy of Sciences has carried with it full membership of the Central Committee. This in itself is indicative of the way in which Central Committee membership appears to reflect the status of the post rather than the qualities of the individual who happens to be filling it at the time.

In the same way as membership of the Central Committee identifies those who constitute the national elite, so regional, city and district committees are composed of those who occupy the most influential positions in the institutions falling within their respective juris-dictions. Just as the national Politburo contains several key figures employed outside the party hierarchy, so too do the party bureaux at the regional and local levels.[8]

As their titles suggest, the party secretariats at national and regional levels are composed exclusively of party officials. Below the regional level there are no separate secretariats; in city and district party organ-isations the secretaries meet in the party bureau.[9] In recent years there have been up to ten secretaries of the Central Committee declining to five at the regional and three at the local level as the spectrum of responsibilities contracts.[10] These officials are served by their own administrative apparatuses. The secretaries of the Central Committee preside over an apparatus consisting of 24 departments, many of which have titles paralleling the principal areas of responsibility sub-ordinated to the USSR Council of Ministers, such as agriculture or construction, while others deal with party matters such as propaganda and internal party management. The number of departments serving the secretaries of subordinate party organisations declines with the diminishing scope of responsibilities to 12 at the regional and four at the district levels.[11]

Science and education have warranted an autonomous department in the Central Committee apparatus at least since the late 1950s. Pre-viously these functions had usually been carried out under the direct supervision of the Propaganda Department and, indeed, science remains under the ultimate authority of the member of the Central Committee Secretariat responsible for these questions.[12] Lower down the hierarchy separate science departments are normally found at the regional level, but they are rarely organised at the city and district levels where science is usually supervised by the third secretary responsible for propaganda and agitation. In cities and districts where particularly important research or higher educational institutions are located, and where scientists are heavily concentrated, it is usual for the first secretary to take a special interest in these affairs.[13] However, in recent years, separate science departments have been set up in the apparatuses of several of the districts into which the Moscow City

Party Organisation is subdivided.[14] Elsewhere science departments run on a part-time basis by locally employed scientific workers are occasionally found assisting party secretaries, as in the case of Obninsk, one of several 'science towns' scattered around the Moscow region.[15]

The party secretaries and those full-time functionaries employed in the apparatus, from the Central Committee down to the district committees, constitute the professional core of the Communist Party. Various attempts have been made to estimate its size, the more recent ones suggesting that there are no more, and probably less, than 100 000 professional functionaries in a party approaching 18 000 000 members.[16]

It is this cadre of officials which manages the internal affairs of the party and supervises the establishments in which the rank-and-file members are employed. It would, therefore, be misleading to regard the electoral procedures, described earlier, as anything more than a guide to the formal structure of the party, for the composition and activities of elected committees and congresses are controlled by central and local party officials. Elections in the Communist Party can best be regarded, therefore, as rituals which coincide with changes in the composition of party organs rather than the means by which these changes are actually made.

COMMUNIST PARTY FUNCTIONS AND NATURAL SCIENTISTS

The functions of the Communist Party touch on all aspects of the working lives of Soviet citizens. In science, as elsewhere, the party supervises political education, vets changes in personnel and intervenes in operational management.

Whilst the party's dominance in the area of political education has never been seriously questioned, the nature and extent of its involvement in the operational management of the economy has aroused critical comments from time to time. As long ago as 1939, a delegate attending the XVIII Congress of the Communist Party observed that the departments of the Central Committee apparatus had 'substituted themselves for economic and soviet organisations and were becoming a peculiar kind of people's commissariat of a people's commissariat'.[17]

More recently Roy Medvedev criticised the role of the Central

Committee apparatus along similar lines. He asserted that as long as a number of industrial and other specialised departments continued to exist in the Central Committee apparatus it would persist in usurping responsibilities properly belonging to the economic and other administrative organs subordinated to the Council of Ministers of the USSR. Medvedev singled out science as a particularly clear example of what he saw as encroachment of the party in the area of 'concrete problems', which might be better left in the hands of the USSR Academy of Sciences and other specialist state agencies. According to Medvedev:

> The Central Committee's large Department of Science and Education not only devotes attention to specific forms of party activity or the general problems of ideological education in scientific and scholarly institutions, but often, to the detriment of these main concerns, tries to decide a great number of concrete problems that would be better dealt with in the Academy of Sciences, the Ministry of Education, the Ministry of Secondary and Higher Specialist Education, or the State Committee on the Co-ordination of Scientific and Technical Research.[18]

The precise nature of the division of labour existing between the departments of the Central Committee apparatus and the ministries and state committees has long remained an area where speculation has tended to outweigh reliable description. There can be little doubt, however, that, as the party's most senior administrative body, the Central Committee apparatus has the power to make independent appraisals of any areas of policy when deemed appropriate. The scope of the apparatus's purview, as reflected in the titles of its departments, is, after all, comprehensive. It is more questionable, in the light of its relatively small size, whether the Central Committee apparatus has the capacity to monitor all important decisions taken by ministries and state committees, in addition to attending to the internal management of the party itself.[19] It may be that the Central Committee intervenes when significant problems arise in the day-to-day operation of state agencies, perhaps acting as a filter through which issues pass en route to the agendas of the Central Committee Secretariat and the Politburo.[20]

Whether these activities are seen as encroachment may depend on the circumstances in which intervention occurs. It could be that the relatively broad opportunities available to scientists for participating in the formulation of science policy, through the general and departmental meetings of the USSR Academy of Sciences and its extensive system of commissions, produce an environment more sensitive to party checks and directives than might be found in other more centralised areas of state administration. Unlike many other institutions, the policy-making bodies of the USSR Academy of Sciences include many people who are primarily neither politicians nor full-time administrators and who are perhaps more likely to question the intervention of external agencies in their professional affairs.

Moving from the formulation to the execution of policy, it has become clear that the Soviet leadership considers that the party has an important role to play in the full range of activities undertaken in scientific research and higher educational institutions. Since the early 1970s party policy has been directed towards increasing the influence of primary organisations in the research establishments of the academies of sciences and the universities. With this object in view a change in the rules of the Communist Party was introduced at the XXIV Congress in 1971 whereby the primary organisations of institutions engaged in fundamental research and academic teaching were given the right to exercise supervision over the administration of these activities.[21] This brought the party rules concerning academic institutions into line with those prevailing virtually everywhere else.

The change was designed to strengthen the influence of primary organisations in the three main functions into which their activities may be divided. These are: political education, the recruitment and deployment of personnel, and the operational management of research. Whilst the activities of primary organisations and the response evoked among scientists is discussed in greater detail in Chapter 7, it is appropriate here to indicate the principal means by which the party influences the working lives of natural scientists in each of these spheres.

The ideological function

The main vehicle for political education among scientists is the methodological or philosophical seminar. Originally such seminars were set up by the Praesidium of the USSR Academy of Sciences to provide a forum for scientists to discuss the broader implications of their work and, in the process, to acquire an appropriately Communist interpretation of their role in Soviet society. During the 1960s these seminars were brought under the direct influence of the party.[22]

Today they are co-ordinated by a special council attached to the Praesidium of the USSR Academy of Sciences. This was set up as a result of encouragement by the Departments of Propaganda and of Science and Educational Institutions of the Central Committee apparatus in 1979.[23] The conduct of the seminars is monitored by the city and district committees of the party through the network of primary organisations located in scientific and academic institutions.[24]

In recent years the number of seminars has grown immensely. In 1970–1 there were some 3700 operating in the whole of the Soviet Union but by 1980 the number had increased by over 60 per cent to more than 6000.[25] At these seminars lectures are delivered and discussions conducted on topics drawn from such general themes as the philosophy of the natural sciences, the works of Lenin, the economic problems of socialism and aspects of current Soviet foreign and domestic policy.[26] Recently much attention has also been paid to the attitude Soviet scientists should adopt to the arms race.[27]

Party functionaries, part-time propagandists and senior scientists may all be found leading these seminars. Over the past few years efforts have been made to organise seminars involving both social and natural scientists in order to bridge the cultural gap between the worlds of science and politics more adequately.[28]

The personnel function

The vetting of those people being considered for appointment to posts with administrative responsibility provides the party with one of its most important means of political control over Soviet society. The list, or _nomenklatura_, of scientific posts requiring the approval of party organs is thought to include the directors of research establishments, their deputies and the heads of the divisions and laboratories into which research establishments are subdivided. Appointment to these posts is thought to require confirmation at the level of the Central Committee apparatus.[29] Although the importance of the _nomenklatura_ system as a means of political control has long been recognised by Western scholars, comparatively little is known about its detailed operation. It would seem, from the fragments of information that appear from time to time, that the system is relatively flexible and subject to change, with posts being incorporated or possibly excluded, or perhaps moved from the responsibility of lower to higher party organs, or vice versa. For example, those social scientists employed in the capital who are in charge of research projects or supervising dissertations in politically sensitive areas have recently been placed in the *nomenklatura* of the Moscow City Party Organisation, whilst those supervising less sensitive dissertations have been placed in the *nomenklatura* of Moscow's district party organisations.[30] From this it would seem to follow that two people holding the same position in the same institution may be included in the *nomenklaturas* of party organs of different levels of seniority.

Where decisions concerning personnel are made by more senior party officials, the role of primary party organisations probably amounts to little more than acting as a conduit through which information may be channelled upwards and instructions handed down. However, primary organisations have the right to be consulted when posts are being filled in scientific research and higher educational establishments, and party spokesmen often claim that primary organisations play an active part in periodically assessing the performance of scientists when contracts of employment are due for renewal.[31] Primary party organisations have been encouraged to regard these activities as an important means of exercising the right to supervise the administration of research establishments and higher educational institutions extended to them at the XXIV Congress.

The managerial function

One of the clearest opportunities for the party to participate in the operational management of research is provided by the socialist competitions. These can assume a variety of forms, from nationwide affairs involving many different institutes to smaller intra-institute competitions in which the performances of laboratories are rated according to their ability to complete projects on time, or improve the qualifications of their staff. In the larger-scale competitions the primary party organisations mobilise the scientists to take on extra tasks, known as 'socialist obligations', which are registered with the city or regional party organisation.[32] Where competition occurs within the institute the results are presented at the meeting of the primary organisation which thereby becomes a forum for discussing the scientific work of the institute.

The desirability of using the meetings of primary party organisations as forums for discussing the substance of research became a regular theme in party publications during the 1970s.[33] The emphasis given to the role of the party in adjudicating research performance has raised the question of whether this has eroded the authority of academic councils of research institutes through which directors exercise operational leadership over their scientists. The question of encroachment by the party is therefore not restricted to interpreting the nature of the relations existing between the departments of the Central Committee apparatus and the ministries and other state agencies, but is also relevant when considering the role of primary party organisations in scientific institutions.

COMMUNIST PARTY MEMBERSHIP AND NATURAL SCIENTISTS

An important indication of the significance attached by the party to the responsibilities carried by any occupational group in Soviet society is the proportion of party members found in its ranks. This is often referred to by Western scholars as the level of 'party saturation'.

In his book on party membership, T. H. Rigby divided up occupational groups into three categories.[34] The first consists of 'party-restricted occupations' and those 'virtually party–restricted', the second of 'high' and the third of 'low' saturation occupations. In addition to full-time party officials and members of government executive bodies, directors of state enterprises, judges and army officers are also members of 'party-restricted' or 'virtually restricted' occupations, where those not in the party account for less than 5 per cent of employees. As one in every two scientific workers possessing the higher degrees of doctor or candidate of sciences is a member of the party, highly qualified scientists and scholars belong to a subgroup which clearly falls into Rigby's category of highly saturated occupations in which the proportion of party members varies from about one in two to one in five.[35] This category also includes government officials and various other kinds of supervisory or professionally qualified personnel. Low saturation occupations, where party membership ranges from around the then national average of one in 12 to much lower levels, are those which require no professional qualifications, confer no managerial or administrative authority, and mostly consist of rank-and-file agricultural and industrial workers.[36]

The relationship between the responsibility of an occupational group and the incidence of party membership observed within its ranks appears, at first glance, to hold unambiguously in the case of scientific workers in possession of higher degrees. Closer inspection, however, shows up a rather more complicated picture. In the first place, the high incidence of party membership among highly qualified scientific workers, taken as a whole and without considering differences between disciplines and institutions, is a comparatively recent phenomenon. In the second place, comparisons between disciplines and institutions, where these are possible, reveal considerable variations in levels of party saturation.

Party membership by academic qualifications and post

If the incidence of party membership among junior and senior scientific workers is compared over several decades it becomes clear, as Rigby has shown, that in the academic world party membership expanded from the bottom up, percolating through to the higher posts only after a considerable period of time had elapsed.[37] During the years of the first five-year plan, for example, party membership among postgraduate students increased much more rapidly than among the teaching and research staffs of institutions of higher education. Among postgraduate students the proportion rose from 9 per cent in 1929–30 to over 45 per cent a year later. Over the same period party membership among the teaching and research staff of higher educational institutions also increased but only from 11 per cent to 13 per cent,[38] whilst in 1930 the overall proportion of party members among scientific workers was reported to be 8 per cent.[39] Subsequent information about party membership among scientific workers in the immediately pre-war period, and during the Second World War itself, is extremely sparse. By 1947, 37 per cent of scientific workers were party members, rising to 40 per cent in 1950 and 43 per cent in 1955.[40]

The inverse relationship between academic status and party membership was especially apparent in the institutes of the USSR Academy of Sciences. On the eve of the war some 50 per cent of junior and 25 per cent of senior scientific workers were party members, in comparison with fewer than 5 per cent of the full and corresponding members of the Academy.[41] By the middle of the 1950s, 33 per cent of full and 39 per cent of corresponding members of the USSR Academy of Sciences were party members.[42] This had increased to 52 per cent of the former and 62 per cent of the latter by 1966, and to 59 per cent and 66 per cent respectively by the mid-1970s.[43] It is noticeable, however, that party saturation has remained higher among those constituting the more junior category of corresponding members than among the full members of the USSR Academy of Sciences.

By the middle of the 1950s the proportion of party members among scientific workers with higher degrees had assumed approximately the same proportions as party membership among the members of the occupational group as a whole. By the beginning of 1956, 44 per cent of scientific workers with higher degrees were party members as against 42 per cent of those without these more advanced qualifications.[44] Since the general disappearance of the inverse relationship between academic status and party membership the earlier situation seems to have been reversed, with those possessing higher degrees becoming more likely to be members of the party than those lacking them. The incidence of party membership among those with higher degrees continued to increase during the latter half of the 1950s; since then a ratio of at least one party member to every two highly qualified scientific workers has persisted (see Table 6.1).

Unfortunately the last year for which national data have been published, giving the level of party membership among all scientific workers and not just those among them possessing higher degrees, was 1955–6. On the basis of the increasing proportions of party members among scientific workers observed during the first half of the 1950s and the subsequent buoyancy of party membership among those with higher degrees, Rigby estimated that the level of party saturation among all scientific workers might have been of the order of 50 per cent by the mid-1960s.[45] Insufficient information has appeared subsequently to check this estimate conclusively but there are grounds for suspecting that the increasing proportion of party membership among scientific workers with higher degrees may not have been matched by a similar increase among those lacking these advanced qualifications.

One source of doubt arises from the very high rate of increase of scientific workers which occurred during the late 1950s and almost throughout the whole of the subsequent decade. By the end of 1969 there were more scientific workers in the Soviet Union with higher degrees than there had been scientific workers of all kinds in 1954.[46] As the overall proportion of highly-qualified scientific workers also fell during these years, from just under 40 per cent to slightly over 25 per cent of the total, it seems that the levels of party membership observed in the early and mid-1950s may not have increased substantially as the number of rank-and-file scientific workers lacking higher degrees rapidly expanded. As science has become a mass profession it seems probable that higher levels of party membership, of 50 per cent or more, may have been reached and maintained only among those qualified for the more responsible jobs. If half of all

TABLE 6.1 Party membership among scientific workers with higher degrees, 1956-7 to 1980 1

	1956-7		1966-7		1976-7		1980 1	
	No. †	Party members ‡ No. and %	No. †	Party members ‡ No. and %	No. †	Party members ‡ No. and %	No. †	Party members ‡ No. and %
Dsc	9761	4026 41.2%	16600	8407 50.6%	34600	22598 65.3%	37700	26181 69.4%
Ksc	85659	37930 44.3%	152400	76640 50.3%	345400	177329 51.3%	396200	203511 51.4%
Total	95420	41956 44.0%	169000	85047 50.3%	380000	199927 52.7%	433900	229692 52.9%

SOURCES *Narodnoe khozyaistvo SSSR v 1956g* (Moscow: Gosstatizdat, 1957) p. 258; *Strana Sovetov za 50 let: sbornik statisticheskikh materialov* (Moscow: Statistika, 1967) p. 283; *Narodnoe khozyaistvo SSSR v 1980g* (Moscow: Finansy i Statistika, 1981) p. 95; 'KPSS v tsifrakh', *Partiinaya zhizn'*, no. 21 (1977) p. 30; 'KPSS v tsifrakh', *Partiinaya zhizn'*, no. 14 (1981) pp. 17–18.

† End of year figures (1956, etc.)

‡ 1 January figures (1957, etc.)

scientists and scholars were assumed to be members of the party today, then it would mean over 4 per cent of all party members would now be drawn from this occupational group alone, by comparison with the 2.5 per cent estimated by Rigby for 1964, thus opening up unprecedented opportunities for intellectual influence within the party.[47]

Some information relating to the level of party saturation among scientific workers employed in Moscow has been published for the early 1970s.[48] It refers to one-fifth of Moscow's communists employed in 'white-collar' occupations (*sluzhashchie–kommunisty*) as being scientific workers. This suggests that about 94 000, or 42 per cent of the 222 600 scientific workers to be found in Moscow at that time, were members of the party.[49] As about a quarter of the Soviet Union's scientific workers are located in the capital, this probably gives a reasonably reliable impression of the national situation. It should also be noted that the level of party membership observed among Moscow's scientific workers in 1970 was virtually the same as the last national figures to be published giving details of party membership among Soviet scientific workers for 1955–6.[50]

Party membership by discipline and type of institution

Comparisons of the levels of party membership observable among different disciplines and institutions show considerable variations. The imbalance in favour of the more politically sensitive social sciences goes back to the 1920s. From the earliest years of Soviet rule it was party policy to train Marxist scholars to replace the historians, philosophers, jurists and others inherited with the pre-revolutionary university faculties, who were considered to be unsympathetic to the Soviet government.

By the end of the 1920s social scientists were already more likely to be party members than natural scientists, but the representation of the party among intellectuals as a whole was still slight. In 1928, for example, only some 678 of the almost 15 000 scientific workers registered in the RSFSR (Russian Soviet Federative Socialist Republic) were party members. The percentages observed varied from 10.3 per cent among social scientists to 3.3 per cent and 1.9 per cent among medical and technical specialists and 1.3 per cent among natural scientists.[51] The uneven distribution among different disciplines appears to have persisted into the post-war years when 58 per cent of social science and philosophy professors were recorded as party members in comparison with 17 per cent of professors of engineering.[52] According to one source, immediately after the war 90 per cent of lecturers in socio-political subjects and two-thirds of economics teachers were members of the party in comparison to one-third of all the permanent teaching staff in Soviet higher education institutions.[53]

Today the bias towards the social sciences in terms of party membership remains clear. In Table 6.2, which shows party membership levels among the staff of six faculties of three universities in 1971, it can be seen that over 90 per cent of those employed in the history faculties and over 60 per cent of those in the psychology faculties were party members, declining to 30 per cent in the case of mathematicians. Overall, the proportion of party members among university lecturers in the early 1970s was 42 per cent.[54]

The proportion of party members among scientific workers with higher degrees employed by the USSR Academy of Sciences was reported to have been 40 per cent in 1970, or about 10 per cent below the national average for scientific workers in possession of these advanced qualifications.[55] However, a considerable degree of regional variation in terms of party membership among scientific workers employed by the USSR Academy of Sciences is suggested by data relating to its Leningrad research institutes.[56] As can be seen from Table 6.3, the level of party membership observed among scientific workers engaged in the different disciplines represented in the Leningrad institutes varied from about 12 per cent to 18 per cent among natural scientists, rising to nearly 33 per cent among social scientists. This last figure is surprisingly low for disciplines which touch on sensitive issues of ideology.

The incidence of party membership clearly increases with advancing qualifications and greater administrative responsibilities, but the more senior positions in research institutes are by no means a party monopoly. Among those occupying the positions of institute director, deputy director, scientific secretary and chiefs of departments, laboratories and sectors in the Leningrad establishments of the USSR Academy of Sciences, 54.4 per cent were party members in 1970. Among rank-and-file senior and junior scientific workers the percentages were 31.1 per cent and 11.6 per cent respectively.[57]

A possible source of explanation for the rather low incidence of party membership among the scientific workers employed in the Leningrad research establishments of the USSR Academy of Sciences, suggested by the incomplete data presented above, is provided by

TABLE 6.2 *Education and party membership of teachers in six faculties in three universities in 1971 (per cent)*

			Faculties			
	Biology	History	Psychology	Physics	Philosophy	Mathematics
Education						
University	63	86	62	60	43	85
Other	37	14	38	40	57	15
Party Membership						
Member of CPSU	40	94	63	43	50	30
Member of Komsomol	2					6

SOURCE Z.F. Esareva, *Osobennosti deyatel'nosti prepodavatelya vysshei shkoly* (Leningrad: izd. LGU, 1974) p. 64.

TABLE 6.3 *Scientific workers of Leningrad institutes of USSR Academy of Sciences by party membership, gender and qualifications in 1970*

	Physico-technical and math. sciences	*Chemico-technical and biological sciences*	*Earth sciences*	*Social sciences*
Percentage of party members	13.0	18.3	12.5	32.6
Percentage of women	29.2	58.6	49.0	47.5
Percentage with higher degrees	52.6	73.2	57.6	67.1

SOURCE Assembled from information cited in *Nauchnye kadry Leningrada* (Leningrad: Nauka, 1973) pp. 51 6.

Jerry Hough, who has pointed out that the rank order of party saturation of different professions reflects the percentages of women found among their members.[58] The percentage of women among the scientific workers employed in the USSR Academy of Sciences' Leningrad institutes in 1970 was about 46 per cent,[59] that is a little higher than the figure for the USSR Academy of Sciences as a whole, but significantly higher than the national average for scientific workers which, at that time, was 38 per cent.[60] However, as Table 6.3 shows, no relationship between the incidence of party membership and the proportion of women represented in different branches of science in the Leningrad institutes can be found. One of the lowest levels of party membership was recorded in the division of physico-technical and mathematical sciences, where the proportion of women was also lowest, whilst the highest incidence of party membership was observed among the social scientists where the proportion of women was considerably higher.

In spite of the significant increases in party representation at the highest levels of the USSR Academy of Sciences, substantial percentages of the full and corresponding members remain outside the party. Considerable differences between disciplines persist, varying from 100 per cent party saturation among full and corresponding members in the fields of philosophy, law and economics to 67 per cent among chemists, 52 per cent among biologists and 46 per cent among physicists and mathematicians.[61]

Although party representation among the members of the Praesidium of the USSR Academy of Sciences is substantially higher than among the full and corresponding members it is not quite the party monopoly which might be expected of a body which functions as an organ of the Soviet government. Also among its members are those who appear to have been co-opted into the party during the later stages of advancement to nationally important positions. For example, the current President of the USSR Academy of Sciences, the veteran physicist A. P. Aleksandrov, did not join the party until 1962, when he was already 59 years old, but within four years he had been elected to full membership of the Central Committee of the Communist Party.[62]

CONCLUSION

A number of conclusions may be drawn from the information on party membership among scientific workers presented in this chapter.

Whilst it is impossible to check Rigby's estimate of 50 per cent party saturation among scientific workers by the mid-1960s thoroughly, the incomplete and circumstantial evidence presented here suggests that this may not have been reached. In contrast to the sparseness of recent reliable data on the level of party membership among scientific workers in general, information continues to be published concerning those in possession of higher degrees. Conceivably this is because of the continued buoyancy of party membership in this category. Here it is noticeable that, while the level of party saturation among those with the less advanced degree of *kandidat nauk* has remained steady at about 50 per cent for nearly two decades, it has risen quite sharply since the mid-1960s among those with doctoral degrees, who are, as a consequence, qualified to fill the most senior academic posts.[63]

Although information concerning levels of party membership among scientific workers in different disciplines is far from comprehensive, what there is consistently shows that, over almost the entire Soviet period, party membership has been significantly higher among those in the politically sensitive social sciences than elsewhere, as would be expected. However, there appear to be considerable variations in the levels of party membership found among the employees of different types of institutions and, in particular, between the research institutes of the USSR Academy of Sciences and the universities. The surprisingly low incidence of party membership among social scientists of the USSR Academy of Sciences' institutes in Leningrad points to what may be a significant general difference in the policy towards party membership among research-orientated Academy scientific workers and lecturers in higher educational institutions, to whose influence students are more directly exposed.

In spite of the elite intellectual status of the USSR Academy of Sciences and its proximity to the centres of power, the level of party membership observed among its more highly-qualified staff falls some way below that of the general category of scientific workers with higher degrees to which they belong. This discrepancy may reflect the combination of distrust and respect displayed by successive generations of Soviet leaders towards scientists and thus may be a further indication that their professional autonomy persists.

7 Communist Party Policy Towards Natural Scientists: Impact and Response

Two principal themes have run through party policy towards the Soviet scientific community since the late 1960s: first, the enhancement of the role of the party in scientific institutions and, second, the pursuit of effective science. Party policy documents and associated commentary in the press assert that these goals are linked in that research can be conducted with maximum efficiency only in scientific research establishments where the influence of the party is strong. In what follows the measures introduced to strengthen the party are analysed and their impact on the working lives of scientists assessed, with the intention of building up a picture of the role of the party in one of the many segments that together compose the total spectrum of its activities.

The emphasis currently placed on the link between the prominence of the party and the effectiveness of research developed in response to the situation confronting Khrushchev's successors. The triumvirate of Brezhnev, Kosygin and Podgorny took over at a time when massive increases in the number of scientific workers, and the entire highly educated stratum of Soviet society, were straining the party's capacity to exercise adequate political control.[1] At the same time the new leaders were concerned to take fresh initiatives to improve the efficiency of the Soviet economy.[2] During the second half of the 1960s it became increasingly clear that advances in science and technology could not continue to be sought by rapidly expanding the numbers of highly-trained manpower.[3] In line with economic strategy as a whole, policy towards science and technology began to shift away from the *extensive* to the *intensive* use of resources in the pursuit of economic growth.[4] In science and technology this change was signified by the deceleration in the rate of expansion of trained personnel, together with an increase in the stress placed on the technical potential of scientific advances as the most significant criterion by which to judge the effectiveness of fundamental research.[5]

The party's role in scientific institutions was examined by investigative commissions set up in the latter half of the 1960s, the findings of which informed a series of decrees aimed at reinvigorating the primary party organisations and increasing their influence on academic life.[6] The problems to be overcome were numerous, even according to the party's own accounts. In the ideological sphere scientists were reported to be unresponsive to political education, often manifesting little knowledge or interest and sometimes turning to the discussion of purely scientific problems of more immediate concern.[7] Many avoided party-sponsored activities, regarding them as a waste of time and an unnecessary incursion into the working day.[8] Accordingly a division of labour was identified between the primary party organisations and the more authoritative scientists who frequently left the bulk of the routine political tasks to the more junior and often ancillary staff.[9] As the 1960s drew to a close scientists began to find themselves under increasing pressure to respond more positively to both the technical and the political demands made by the party leadership.

Whilst many scientists were politically agnostic or aloof, others developed more explicitly critical responses to their circumstances. The party press began to identify symptoms of 'humanism' and 'liberalism' which were duly condemned.[10] Measures taken by the party to counter the spread of what were regarded as 'bourgeois' ideologies suggested that these ideas exerted a powerful attraction on the younger generation of scientists who had been students during the 'thaw' and had been exposed to the criticisms of Stalin and the fresh ideas which circulated at that time.

In science the relaxation under Khrushchev had permitted the expansion of professional autonomy which had been expressed in a variety of ways. During the early 1960s the traditional commitment of the academies of sciences to fundamental research was successfully reasserted with the transfer of most of their more technically-orientated research establishments to industry.[11] At the same time resistance became more explicit to the anomalous persistence of political interference in scientific theories which was sustained, in the case of genetics, by Khrushchev's continuing support for Lysenko.[12] Some scientists also took steps to influence the way in which their discoveries were being used, thereby stepping beyond the strictly scientific and into other areas of policy. Notable here was the pressure exerted by leading physicists opposed to the atmospheric testing of nuclear devices.[13]

The defence or deployment of professional autonomy could thus easily develop into a more thorough-going critique of the Stalinist legacy or lead to demands for more general democratisation. Both of these clearly breached the shadowy line between tolerated professional opinion and proscribed political comment. Such unacceptable ideas became prominent themes in the *samizdat* literature which grew in volume when restrictions on the freedom of expression increased in severity as the 1960s drew to a close. The large volume of *samizdat* itself provided the party with daily evidence of the credibility gap existing between official propaganda and the ideas circulating among the intelligentsia.[14]

By the end of the decade a reform of the planning system in science had been introduced to provide a framework within which scientific research could be made to become more responsive to the technical needs of production.[15] By the beginning of the 1970s a strategy designed to enhance the influence of the party in science and higher education had begun to take shape. According to the party's logic this was necessary to provide the basis for the realisation of the nation's scientific and technical potential.

ENHANCING THE PARTY'S ROLE IN SCIENCE: THE LEBEDEV DECREE AND THE RIGHT OF PARTY SUPERVISION

The Soviet leadership's belief that effective research could be achieved in full measure only in institutions strongly influenced by the party was expressed most forcefully in a decree published in September 1970, in which the Central Committee comprehensively criticised the performance of the primary party organisation of the nation's most prestigious research establishment in physics, the Lebedev Physics Institute of the USSR Academy of Sciences.[16] The Institute's party committee was censured for failing to carry out adequate political education work, for exerting insufficient influence on the deployment of personnel within the Institute, and for playing an insufficiently prominent part in the conduct of research, the quality of which was claimed to have been impaired as a consequence.

These criticisms concerned the three principal areas of party responsibility: political education, personnel control and the operational management of research itself. The decree instructed the party organisation to consider the improvement of the standard of political education as its chief task, emphasising that scientists should be made to feel the need to study Marxism-Leninism, to contribute to party propaganda and to reject the 'idealistic' opinions attributed to bourgeois scientists. With regard to the control of personnel, the party committee was instructed to promote young scientists who had proved themselves to be both scientifically *and* politically sound to the more responsible posts within the institute, and to recruit them into the party along with authoritative older scientists. The Central Committee's instructions on the appropriate role of the party organisation in actual research work were less specific than those concerning political education or personnel control: the organisation should assume greater responsibility for the conduct of research and supplement the existing programme by mounting a 'large-scale' socialist competition to salute the XXIV Party Congress, then six months away.

Taken as a whole the decree criticised the party organisation for being peripheral to the intellectual life of the Lebedev Institute and for showing little enthusiasm for enhancing its influence. Whilst many other institutes might have been chosen as examples, the selection of the Lebedev Institute may have been influenced by the presence of Andrei Sakharov among its staff. Sakharov had been offered employment in the Institute in 1969, following the withdrawal of his security clearance after the publication abroad of his book entitled *Progress, Coexistence and Intellectual Freedom*, a work which epitomised the allegedly 'bourgeois' values criticised so sharply in the Soviet press at this time.[17] The general relevance of this decree, should it be thought that it related exclusively to the Lebedev Institute and Sakharov's influence therein, was emphasised by the secretary of the Institute's party committee, who commented at the time:

I want to stress that, in my opinion, the decree does not only concern us. At various times I have had occasion to get to know other scientific establishments and it seems to me that these party organisations will see themselves in many of the Central Committee's conclusions. In short, this document is another expression of the party's concern for the development of science.[18]

This interpretation was confirmed by a series of subsequent party decisions designed to enhance the role of the party in all establishments concerned with scientific research and academic teaching. The first of these was introduced at the XXIV Party Congress when changes were announced in the party rules.[19] The powers of primary party organisations in scientific research and academic teaching institutions were enhanced to bring them into line with those in industry. Specifically, primary organisations were given the right to supervise the administration of scientific and scholarly institutions in which they operated. This meant that they were now empowered to check whether the decisions taken by the academic council of a research or higher education institution fully accorded with the instructions of higher party organs. The amendment to the party rules clearly demonstrated the party leadership's desire to place the expanded role of the party in science, envisaged in the decree on the Lebedev Institute, on a sound 'constitutional' footing, and thus lend additional authority to the attempt to overcome the division of labour which had been allowed to persist between science and politics.

However, it should also be noted that the change in the party rules did not concern natural scientists alone. It referred to all aspects of academic teaching and research and thus affected primary party organisations throughout the academies of sciences and the universities. As such it may be regarded as a response to the dissatisfaction felt by the party leadership with the level of party control exercised over the intelligentsia as a whole, which surfaced in public criticism of the social sciences and the performing arts as well as the natural sciences.[20]

ENHANCING THE ROLE OF THE PARTY IN HIGHER EDUCATION

Parallel measures to step up the influence of the party in higher educational establishments were at the heart of several decrees, introduced between mid-1972 and the end of 1974, which were intended to improve both academic standards and the level of political reliability of staff and students. The first decree, issued on the joint authority of the Central Committee and the USSR Council of Ministers, not only required the USSR Ministry of Higher and Secondary Specialised Education to take steps to raise the academic quality of teaching staff but also criticised local party organs for failing to exert sufficient control over their selection and deployment.

The ministry was required to work out new regulations on the filling of academic posts, reflecting the Central Committee's concern to enhance the level of political reliability required of staff. Throughout the decree political criteria were assigned weight at least equal to academic standards. The intention of expanding the role of the party in higher education was clearly stated in the instruction to subordinate party organs 'to direct the activities of primary party organisations and the collectives of institutions of higher education in further improving the training and communist education of future specialists, and to strengthen the influence of the party in all sectors of higher educational institutions'.[21]

The implications of this injunction were elaborated in two subsequent decrees which indicated that the Central Committee intended exercising greater control over the substance of science teaching as well as the recruitment and deployment of teachers. In the summer of 1973, the Central Committee revealed the importance it attached to increasing the political component in science courses when it instructed the staff of the Leningrad Polytechnical Institute 'to expose more profoundly the ideological content of general science and specialist subjects' and to pay greater attention to the acquisition by students of the values considered by the party leadership as appropriate for future Soviet scientists.[22]

Not long after the publication of this decree a party official stressed that the task of political education was the responsibility not only of teachers of the social sciences but of everyone involved in education, regardless of their specialisation. He stated that the party committee of one of Moscow's leading teaching establishments, the Bauman Higher Technical School, had been investigating the content of some of its specialised courses and this had revealed that, as a rule, teachers considered the broader political implications of their disciplines only in the introductory lecture of their courses, after which such questions were generally ignored. Plans for courses in scientific and specialist disciplines should, he urged, clearly define a pattern of political education running right through the teaching of these subjects.[23]

The following year these issues resurfaced in a further Central Committee decree naming the Bauman Higher Technical School together with the University of Saratov. It proposed measures to improve the quality of teaching in the social sciences and to increase the impact of these subjects throughout the higher educational system, including courses in science and technology.[24]

Signs of the failure on the part of the party to generate much enthusiasm among students for courses in political education and associated political activities were just as clear as in the case of scientists. Evidence of this surfaced in sociological investigations of both students and academic staff who, like their counterparts in research establishments, tended to regard party activities as an impediment to their work.[25] Party officials admitted that political education programmes sometimes lacked purpose and often failed to harmonise with other higher educational courses thereby provoking a purely formal response from the students.[26]

These weaknesses were recognised by the Central Committee's criticisms of the Bauman Higher Technical School and Saratov University, which stated that lectures in the political education programme were superficial and failed to provide convincing criticisms of 'bourgeois theories'. In line with the earlier decree, which named the Leningrad Polytechnical Institute, it was pointed out that ideological issues had not become an integral part of lectures at either the Bauman School or Saratov University.[27] The party committees and the responsible officials of both institutions were duly instructed to take energetic measures to eradicate these defects.

Of all the decisions affecting Soviet academic life taken in the 1970s perhaps the most significant concerned the reform of the system of awarding higher degrees and academic titles. The implications of this reform spread far beyond higher educational establishments to affect the staff of all research institutions as well. In autumn 1974, the Central Committee and the USSR Council of Ministers jointly issued a decree which stated that the USSR Higher Attestation Commission, the body charged with confirming the award of higher degrees and academic titles, had lost the capacity to supervise the academic councils of the numerous higher educational and research establishments which possessed the right to adjudicate submissions for higher degrees.[28] The publication of the decree was preceded by the appearance in the Soviet press of a number of articles which graphically described the symptoms of the loss of control. Cases of blatant plagiarism were cited; and instances where the rules governing the composition of councils had not been adhered to were said to have been frequent.[29]

The importance attached by the political leadership to tightening up the system of awarding higher degrees and titles was shown by the transfer of the Higher Attestation Commission from the auspices of the USSR Ministry of Higher and Secondary Specialised Education to those of the USSR Council of Ministers. This broke an association going back to the early 1930s. Whilst there can be little doubt about the seriousness of the attempt to improve academic standards,[30] political criteria were by no means ignored. The decree laid down that an 'immutable rule' be established according to which only dissertations considered to be of scientific and practical value, submitted by people who had proved their worth in scientific and production *and* public work, would be considered.[31] The reference to public work meant that the criterion of political reliability was explicitly introduced into the system of awarding higher degrees which are the gateway to all elite positions in the Soviet academic hierarchy.

PARTY POLICY SUMMARISED

The theme of enhancing the role of primary party organisations assumed a prominent place in decisions concerning science and higher education taken during the first half of the 1970s. This was presented as a precondition for the achievement of an efficient system of scientific research which would be more closely geared to meeting the technical demands of the economy.

From 1970 onwards a series of measures was introduced intended to integrate primary party organisations into the running of all aspects of science and higher education, including the operational management of research and the conduct of academic teaching. In order to overcome the division of labour between science and politics a greater overlap was sought between the members of party committees and bureaux, and the academic councils of institutes and higher educational institutions. Only then could primary party organisations be credibly presented as the authentic forums of decision-making in academic institutions. To achieve this, party committees were instructed to attempt to recruit authoritative scientists and youthful talent, a move facilitated by the decision to make political reliability an explicit criterion when awarding advanced qualifications necessary for career advancement in science.

These decisions were designed not only to enhance the party's organisational weight in the academic sphere but also to influence the direction of research and the character of teaching. It was hoped that, as the influence of the party expanded, research would become both more effective and more readily influenced by the practical needs of production. In this way the party could achieve the more tangible role in science which had previously eluded it, and also benefit from the prestige associated with scientific and technical advance.

THE RESPONSE TO PARTY POLICY

The policies introduced by the Central Committee during the earlier part of the 1970s were applied with varying degrees of success. The evidence suggests that the quality of the party committees and bureaux of primary organisations in scientific establishments improved during the decade as a result of some success in recruiting more highly-qualified scientific workers. Between 1972 and 1980 the proportion of those holding the advanced degree of doctor of sciences who were members of the party increased from 59 per cent to 69 per cent.[32] Party officials working in districts where scientific and higher educational institutions are concentrated reported increases in the percentage of members of primary party organisations who held the degree of either doctor or candidate of sciences. Generally the figure of 70 per cent was mentioned, which indicated an increase of some 10 per cent in less than a decade.[33]

Whether these numerical improvements represented an increase in the influence of the party organisations in research and higher educational institutions is more difficult to assess. Party officials, not surprisingly, have tended to emphasise the positive impact of the policy. They cite cases where city and district officials have successfully intervened in the affairs of research institutes said to have been performing inadequately. Such accounts often describe how research projects were rationalised and reorientated towards practical goals as scientists were made more aware of their political responsibilities. As a result of monitoring the introduction of measures such as these, the roles of the primary party organisations of the research institutes involved were reported to have assumed greater prominence, whilst the scientists became more politically conscious and the research more useful.[34]

Such accounts, however, also describe problems encountered by primary organisations when attempting to utilise the right of supervision granted to them at the XXIV Party Congress of 1971. Difficulties have arisen from the fact that party bodies have attempted to take over functions hitherto carried out by responsible scientific bodies alone. The result has been conflict, duplication and confusion.[35] Whilst some primary party organisations have been instructed not to try to dictate to academic councils, others have been rebuked for refusing to take on academic responsibilities. On occasion dilemmas have been resolved by subterfuge when party secretaries have concocted agendas of meetings to create the impression of vigorous involvement in the running of science.[36]

These kinds of tension are probably less seriously felt in those institutions where the membership of the party committee or bureau overlaps extensively with that of the academic council and incorporates most of those occupying responsible posts in the academic hierarchy. However, where this occurs it can result in the practice of one committee supervising another when both consist of virtually the same people. Alternatively, in those instances where party committees lack authoritative scientists, they may depend for their information and guidance on the very people whose activities they are meant to be supervising.[37] The proliferation of commissions set up since 1971 to help primary party organisations exercise the right of supervision seems likely to have increased the pressure of administrative tasks on scientists' time. If this has occurred it will have been as a direct consequence of policies introduced to increase the efficiency of research and higher education by enhancing the influence of the party in these spheres.

Persistent difficulties have also been experienced in the area of ideology. As Marxism-Leninism provides the justification for the attempt to establish a prominent role for the party in scientific research and higher educational institutions, the seriousness of the party's seeming failure to generate a positive response from scientists is readily apparent. Essentially the party leadership wants scientists to illustrate the assertion that Soviet society provides a uniquely accommodating environment for the advancement of science and the exploitation of the technologies flowing from it. According to the party this arises from the unique compatibility said to exist between the methodologies of the natural sciences and Marxism-Leninism.[38] Natural scientists are thus encouraged to interpret scientific advances to illustrate this claim by emphasising the role played by the party in generating a creative atmosphere in research establishments.[39]

During the 1970s the contribution made by Soviet natural scientists to the party's propaganda effort fell short of expectations. Party officials reported that scientists frequently lacked the knowledge and the inclination to bridge the gap between science and politics. Where this occurred scientists could not be depended on to dismiss political views at odds with those laid down by the party.[40]

The uncertain performance of the party in carrying out programmes of political education has been explained in a variety of related ways.

For many years scientists have been regarded as especially vulnerable to the foreign influences associated with the international character of their disciplines. In contrast to the situation prevailing in the social sciences, which are still officially regarded as vehicles for the elaboration of ideology,[41] the belief that theories in the natural sciences are substantively affected by differences of political environment has ceased to exert much influence in the Soviet Union.[42] However, the party apparatus's sensitivity to the possibility that natural scientists may, in the course of their professional communications, become exposed to unacceptable political ideas, in addition to the permitted scientific ones, is demonstrated by the limitations still imposed on contacts between Soviet scientists and their colleagues abroad and by the concern to make the Soviet propaganda message more palatable.

In addition to the susceptibilities of scientists arising from the inherent character of the natural sciences, an explanation of the deficiencies of the Soviet propaganda effort has been sought in the questionable quality of the party's political education programme itself. Although primary party organisations have received regular official reminders of the need to reinvigorate the dissemination of propaganda, sharp criticism has also been directed at the social sciences which provide much of the substance of the Soviet propaganda effort. Soviet leaders require that the unique compatibility they claim exists between science and ideology be credibly demonstrated, and much of the responsibility for this task falls on Soviet social scientists.[43]

Following the Central Committee's specific criticisms of the teaching of the social sciences at the Bauman Higher Technical School and Saratov University in 1974, attention has been paid by party officials to improving the overall quality of social scientists and to increasing their influence in higher educational institutions and in the conduct of methodological seminars, which are the main vehicle for political education of natural scientists. Although strenuous steps have been taken, especially in Moscow, to bring natural and social scientists together in programmes of jointly organised seminars, doubts remain about the political soundness of the social as well as the natural scientists. Social scientists have been criticised for accomplishing little in elaborating such pivotal concepts in contemporary Marxist-Leninist theorising as 'developed socialism', which is the stage through which the Soviet Union is said to be currently passing. The success of the party's effort to improve the credibility of its political education programmes for natural scientists has, therefore, been limited not only by the difficulties arising from the theoretical independence of the natural sciences but also by the inadequacies of those responsible for developing the programmes themselves.[44]

PERSISTING PROBLEMS: PARTY POLICY IN THE LATE 1970s AND 1980s

The seriousness of the party's shortcomings in controlling scientists and, in particular, the deficiencies of the political education system, were placed in a national perspective by a decree published in April 1979 in which the Central Committee criticised the Soviet propaganda effort as a whole in the most uncompromising terms.[45] The system's most important weakness was its failure to measure up to the requirements of an increasingly educated public, a defect to which the scientific intelligentsia might be expected to respond with particular sensitivity. This weakness was manifested in the 'dread' with which propagandists were said to regard the open discussion of genuinely urgent issues and their tendency to 'smooth over' and 'by-pass' unresolved problems and tricky questions.

Harshest criticism was reserved for the manner in which Marxism-Leninism was presented. The effectiveness of political education was reported to have been seriously impaired by 'formalism and a susceptibility to wordy twaddle and all kinds of propaganda clichés, a dull, trite style of material and the recurrent repetition of general truths'. These failings were linked to the persistence of phenomena described as 'inimical to socialism' which ranged from bribery to bureaucracy and from heavy drinking to hooliganism. Party organisations were, once again, told to regard the improvement of ideological work as their paramount task.

In spite of its uncompromising language, the decree did not question the 'general truths' which constitute the substance of Marxism-Leninism but the manner in which they were being interpreted and disseminated. In science the truths given special prominence include the assertion that Soviet society provides the most accommodating environment in which to conduct research and, following from this, that a prominent role for the party in science is a prerequisite for effective research.

In the past Soviet scientists who have publicly questioned these kinds of assertions have usually placed their careers in jeopardy and found themselves classified as dissidents. Yet it is widely appreciated among Soviet scientists that although the state funds research generously and publicly honours scientists, the party, by virtue of its political supremacy, cannot avoid its share of responsibility for the shortages of equipment, blockages in communication channels and hold-ups in the economic exploitation of new technologies which continue to impair the Soviet scientific effort.

The assertion that strong party influence over scientific institutions is a prerequisite for effective research is thus difficult to sustain. There may be some credence in the party's claims to help with the co-ordination of research projects or with the motivation of staff. However, some of the problems which the party claims to solve are of its own making in that political controls tend to reduce the influence of international scientific networks in Soviet scientific institutions, and in so doing reduce the effectiveness of communications and blunt the motivating force of broad professional recognition. A clash between political and professional values may also be observed in the procedures for appointing scientific staff. This is one of the areas in which the right of supervision has been most extensively exercised by the primary party organisations. Here the difficulty arises of reconciling the party's claim to be aiding effective research with the denial of promotion to scientific talent on political grounds.[46]

It is difficult to identify a role for the party in research which grows naturally out of the professional relations of scientists and their associated needs to communicate relatively freely, to define their tasks with some measure of independence from external pressures and to develop working relationships which cross institutional and, often, national boundaries. Instead of recognising these requirements as the necessary means of conducting research successfully, the party regards them as privileges to be granted to those who can demonstrate their political reliability as well as, and sometimes instead of, their scientific worth.

The impression that the party's contribution to the practical management of scientific establishments is to a considerable degree synthetic, in that it functions in response to instructions from above rather than to genuine needs arising in the course of research, is supported by the regularity with which superior party organs have had to intervene to straighten out subordinate committees and bureaux. The dwindling impact of party instructions in science has been captured in an appropriately scientific simile used by a party official when he noted that 'The fate of these undertakings is reminiscent of a phenomenon in physics where oscillation fades in accordance with the distance from the source'.[47] The persisting need to combat such 'fade' has been demonstrated by two further decrees issued by the Central Committee in 1977 and 1980 which criticised, respectively, the Siberian Division and the Far Eastern Scientific Centre of the USSR Academy of Sciences.[48] Once again party organisations were criticised for inactivity in the areas of ideological education, personnel control and operational management in which their influence was supposed to have been expanding. Party organs from the provincial and regional committees down to the primary organisations were instructed to strengthen their influence in all areas of the administration of research with a view to improving the efficiency of research, the quality of staff and the level of the moral and political education to which they were exposed.

CONCLUSION: THE INCOMPATIBILITY OF PARTY GOALS

The basic premise of party policy towards scientists, which states that research can only be conducted with maximum effectiveness in institutions where the influence of the party is strong, cannot be sustained in the face of much evidence to the contrary. Rather than encouraging conditions conducive to creativity the party apparatus, acting through the primary organisations of scientific establishments, tends to undermine them. Limitations on foreign travel and other forms of international communication obstruct the free flow of information and frustrate the development of informal networks of researchers which play important roles in identifying problems and allocating professional recognition for their successful solution. The introduction of political judgements in the process of making academic appointments and awarding higher degrees further reduces the impact of professionally recognised talent in Soviet scientific institutions by diluting the academic content of the criteria in terms of which an individual's performance may be assessed and career prospects determined.

Many of the functions carried out by primary party organisations in scientific establishments, such as the conduct of political education and the vetting of appointments, have not developed in response to day-to-day requirements in managing research projects but were introduced on the instructions of superior party organs. In those areas where primary party organisations attempt to participate directly in the operational management of research, they appear to be either duplicating activities already being carried out by the scientific leadership or compensating for some of the negative consequences of the system of political control of which they themselves are the agents.

It may be concluded that the party's relative success in expanding its role in scientific research and higher educational establishments during the 1970s has been based mainly on increasing the significance of externally imposed political criteria in evaluating the performance of scientists. The prominence of the party has been sustained not by the spontaneous support of the scientific community, but by the periodic reapplication of pressure from superior party organs, ultimately the Central Committee.

8 Conclusion: Science and the Centralised State

UNIVERSAL SCIENCE – INSULATED SCIENTISTS

After the death of Stalin the notion that there could be a peculiarly socialist science lost ground. Under Khrushchev the situation became ambiguous. Whilst international links severed under Stalin began to be slowly reformed, Khrushchev's personal support for Lysenkoite genetics reimposed a division between Soviet and world science in this field, a situation reminiscent of that which existed in the late 1940s. Since Khrushchev, it has generally been the case that Soviet leaders have accepted the universal nature of the natural sciences.

The Soviet political leadership has not yet fully come to terms with the consequences of their recognition that knowledge about the natural world transcends ideological differences. For if the natural sciences are considered universal, then it has also to be recognised that scientists engaged in the same kinds of research are unlikely to be contained exclusively within the boundaries of either the socialist or capitalist systems. Under Brezhnev, policy towards scientists failed to come to grips with the implications of the international division of labour in the natural sciences and most of the barriers obstructing the co–operation between Soviet scientists and their Western counterparts remained in place.

This ambiguity was rationalised by a formula which distinguished between the cognitive and social aspects of science. Whilst the natural sciences were recognised as universal and thus theoretically autonomous, differences in the socialist or capitalist environments in which research is conducted were said to provide special benefits for and impose particular political responsibilities on Soviet scientists. As Soviet socialism is claimed to provide an environment in which science can be advanced more rapidly and its technical benefits exploited more humanely than elsewhere, it follows that Soviet scientists have no reason to criticise the state which nurtures their efforts so gen-

97

erously. In this they are contrasted with their Western counterparts among whom doubts about the commercial and military exploitation of their work are to be regarded as an enlightened response to contemporary capitalism.

In practical terms the consequences of the party's resistance to the implications of the international division of labour in science are less benign for the Soviet scientist than those portrayed in the propaganda. Although the relative flexibility extended to Soviet scientific institutions is a response to the inherently decentralised character of the scientific system, centralised planning and political controls administered through the Communist Party continue to inhibit the effective functioning of science in the USSR.

Limitations imposed on the development of working relations between Soviet scientists and their colleagues abroad minimise the overlap between Soviet and international networks of informally communicating scientists. As a result the Soviet fundamental research effort does not benefit from the rapid transmission of comprehensive information about developments in the rest of the world. Soviet policy-making organs in science are not as sensitive to the emergence of problems considered significant in the West and Soviet scientists only experience the stimulus of international recognition in a muted form. Rather than exploiting the potential for improving the management of research in the USSR by opening it up to the self-regulating mechanisms of international scientific communities, their influence is resisted and remains restricted.

In consequence the Soviet scientific community is weakened, and the management of scientific research is thus more open to the influence of priorities arising outside science in the economy and defence. Through the operation of the centralised planning system, the Soviet academies of sciences are subject to systematic pressure to undertake technical projects which do not always allow for research of scientific significance to be undertaken. Although the scientific worth of fundamental research can only be judged initially in terms of the recognition it receives in the international scientific community, the performance of the Soviet academy system is also evaluated in terms of the contribution it makes to more immediately practical requirements. Whilst it is generally recognised that the technical potential of scientific advances may take many years to appear, it would seem that, through the introduction of special-purpose planning, more concrete technical proposals are likely to be required from fundamental research establishments before resources are released. This may make it more difficult to accommodate research of potential scientific significance which lacks obvious technical promise.

THE ROLE OF THE PARTY

From the assertion that science flourishes in the Soviet Union it follows that the party, as its leading institution, can only influence the research and higher educational systems in a positive way. However, the primary party organisation in the scientific research establishment or higher educational institution does not draw its authority from informal research communities, for the relations contained within these crosscut the formal hierarchies through which party control is exercised. Instead the authority of the primary party organisation derives from the party apparatus which it serves. As a consequence, the self-regulating role of research communities, whereby information is exchanged, priorities set and professional recognition distributed without recourse to centralised political authority is an anathema to a hierarchical organisation such as the party, the functions of whose local organs include the verification of instructions and the vetting of appointments in terms of centrally determined criteria.

The credibility of the party's claim to foster conditions conducive to effective science rests to a significant degree on its efforts to compensate for the muted influence of informal scientific networks. Hence the party's emphasis on its role in motivating scientists and co-ordinating research reflects the degree to which political controls suppress the professional mechanisms which would otherwise meet these needs. The official image of the role played by the party in science is also dependent on the underlying threat of coercion, in the sense that those Soviet scientists who have questioned the credibility of this interpretation have faced sanctions of varying degrees of severity. The first level of sanctions visited upon Soviet scientists who have transgressed in this way is usually the withdrawal of the possibility of working abroad. This is almost a reflex response to any blemish entered on an individual's record. In this way the opportunity to build a scientific reputation today is dependent upon the scientist accepting in silence those restrictions on international communication which are damaging to science in the USSR. Instead of treating free access to the means of direct and regular personal communication as a general requirement of scientists it is granted as an individual privilege. An important means of increasing the effectiveness of science as a whole in the USSR is thus used as an inducement to guarantee individual political conformity.

SOURCES OF CHANGE

Whilst the barriers to international scientific exchange remained in place during the 1970s, signs that they were being lowered more frequently and that slow progress was being made towards the integration of science in the Soviet Union and in the rest of the world were detected. Zhores Medvedev, for example, gained the impression that by the mid-1970s more Soviet scientists, at least in certain fields, were attending conferences abroad than had previously been the case, and that this was accompanied by a significant increase in the number of articles written by Soviet scientists being published by international journals.[1]

In the 1980s authoritative recognition has been forthcoming of the need to further this process. For example, Academician Ovchinnikov has recently observed:

Contemporary science cannot be successfully developed if it is locked in the boundaries of one country. Many scientific problems have a global character. Only correct assessment of the state of affairs in different countries and regions can give the optimal solution to global problems. But even the particular, concrete problems of physics, chemistry and biology cannot, today, be successfully resolved by the scientists of one country without contacts with the scientists of other countries. World science possesses immense potential in each branch of knowledge, so many scientific collectives are working that, without the exchange of information, the economical organisation of the scientist's work is simply impossible. The exchange of information simply increases the effectiveness of this work.[2]

In his capacity as Chairman of the Council for Philosophical Seminars attached to the Praesidium of the USSR Academy of Sciences, Ovchinnikov shoulders considerable responsibility for the political education of Soviet scientists. As mentioned earlier, this Council was set up as a result of the encouragement of the Central Committee's Departments of Propaganda and of Science and Educational Institutions. It is not surprising, therefore, that

Ovchinnikov also emphasised the continuing need for implacability on the part of Soviet scientists in the struggle with bourgeois ideology. It seems probable that any further expansion of contacts between Soviet and foreign scientists would be accompanied by fresh efforts to ensure their political reliability.

However, ideological conflict arising from the greater integration of Soviet scientists into the world scientific community may not in fact face the party with the strongest challenge to its role in science. Accepting the implications of an international division of scientific labour may present the greater threat to the party's role. If Soviet scientists become increasingly involved in international scientific networks, the development of fundamental research in the Soviet Union is likely to become more directly influenced by the criteria of scientific significance than those reflecting domestic technical needs. Any reduction in the importance of external technical criteria in assessing the performance of Soviet scientists would, in turn, reduce the significance of the verification function performed by the party in science.

Increasing the exposure of Soviet research to international standards would help to motivate Soviet scientists and also provide a clearer means of assessing their quality. International recognition would become a more realistic incentive, and exposure to world standards would discriminate between different levels of talent more precisely than is currently possible. As a consequence various traditional incentive schemes organised by the party in the form of socialist competitions might have to be rethought, and discrepancies between the political and professional qualities of scientists, sustained in Soviet hierarchies by the *nomenklatura* system, could become more embarrassing.

Finally, and perhaps most importantly, Soviet citizens would be involved in co-operative working arrangements not contained within the socialist system and thus not fully under party control. If substantial numbers of Soviet scientists were to participate in international scientific networks on a regular basis, the centralised party would be faced with a new departure in the professional pluralisation which Soviet society has been undergoing since Stalin. In science, the party would have to adjust to an environment influenced by the operation of numerous groups, many of the members of which would be outside its political control.

The greater exposure of Soviet scientists to their foreign colleagues might, therefore, be expected to highlight the problems which already

exist for the party in carrying out its right to supervise the administration of research establishments and higher educational institutions.
Its role in the operational management of research, which already
duplicates that of the academic councils, would appear even more
superfluous, while the system of subjecting personnel to political
vetting would seem more arbitrary as it became increasingly visible to
the outside world.

In the light of what Ovchinnikov has said, it would seem unlikely
that any significant increase in the exposure of Soviet scientists to
foreign influences would be permitted without attempting to
strengthen the party's ideological role in order to improve scientists'
political reliability. However, the party's ability to maintain the
credibility of its political education programme in science is substantially dependent on the buoyancy of its organisational role in
supervising the operational management of science and, in particular,
its ability to encourage or obstruct the careers of individual scientists.
If the capacity of primary party organisations to exercise their rights
of supervision were to be weakened as a result of an increase in the
influence of international scientific networks, attempts to tighten up
ideological control in an effort to compensate might appear especially
intrusive and could lead to fresh outbreaks of dissent.

The contradiction in party policy towards science between the desire
for effective research on the one hand and for reliable, ideologically
committed scientists on the other, seems unlikely to diminish as Soviet
leaders become increasingly aware that the potential of the Soviet
fundamental research effort cannot be achieved in isolation from
developments elsewhere in the world.

SCIENCE AND POLITICAL REFORM

It is now over 20 years since any major reforms of the party structure
were attempted. The measures introduced under Khrushchev in the
early 1960s were designed to limit the tenure of those sitting on party
committees and to improve the quality of the party's supervision over
the economy by dividing the regional and local party apparatuses into
industrial and agricultural sectors.[3] The opposition these measures
aroused is generally assigned importance in accounting for
Khrushchev's removal in the autumn of 1964. Indeed both reforms
were quickly reversed by his successors.[4]

In the three decades since Stalin's death, Soviet society has

undergone considerable changes. A predominantly rural, unsoph-
isticated population has become urbanised, educated and pro-
fessionalised. These and many accompanying developments have been
absorbed by the party, the membership of which is selected to reflect
the broad spectrum of occupational groups into which the Soviet
population is divided.[5]

It has been admitted by the party leadership, with unusual candour,
that the party's methods of disseminating ideology have failed to meet
the requirements of this increasingly sophisticated population.[6] No
such inadequacies have so far been discussed concerning the party's
organisational role, although differences of emphasis have been
detected among leading members of the Politburo by Western
scholars.[7] However, as the preceding chapters have suggested, there
are grounds for believing that difficulties exist for the party in supervising the administration of scientific institutions of at least equal
seriousness to those already recognised in the ideological sphere.

In science this manifests itself in the duplication of the management
of research institutes by party commissions with the result that the
functions performed by primary organisations have a tendency to
atrophy. When this has become conspicuous the Central Committee
has issued decrees criticising specific institutions, such as the Lebedev
Physics Institute, the Bauman Higher Technical School and the research
establishments of the USSR Academy of Sciences' Siberian Division.
Although decrees such as these have stimulated an immediate increase
in the level of party activity in science, the frequency with which they
are repeated suggests that their effectiveness soon wears off.

Problems of this kind are not exclusive to academic life. In all
branches of employment involving specialised knowledge and sophisticated techniques, the question arises as to what party supervision
means. It has been pointed out by Moshe Lewin, for example, that the
local apparatuses of the party are frequently left to supervise the
unskilled sections of the labour force, being ill-equipped to judge the
competence of the technical staff or to make a genuine contribution to
the kind of problems they may encounter in their work.[8]

He has also argued that the party has failed to come to terms with
the pluralisation of the work force in spite of its careful steps to
maintain the representativeness of its membership.[9] This is especially
apparent in the case of professions in the sphere of science and
technology, where the nature of the work requires the delegation of
authority and the observance of independent technical standards in
operational management. The centralised structure and authoritarian

style of the party apparatus renders it incompatible with many aspects of the working situations it claims to supervise. The party apparatus is therefore inadequately equipped to respond to the needs of rank-and-file membership among whom an increasingly large proportion are professionally qualified.[10]

Proposals made by Roy Medvedev concerning the reform of the party structure throw further light on this question.[11] Underpinning his suggestions was the realisation of how the relationship between the party apparatus and the primary party organisations prevented the latter from exerting any significant collective influence on the party hierarchy. Because primary party organisations are organised in the place of work, whilst the apparatus is organised on a territorial basis, the chances of workers in a particular branch of industry, or the members of the same profession, being able to bring collective influence to bear on the district party committee and its professional functionaries are minimised. This will only rarely be achieved. It may occur to some extent in areas where there are especially high concentrations of particular types of jobs, as is in fact the case with scientific workers in some of the districts into which the Moscow City Party Organisation is subdivided.[12] Generally the impact of opinions or complaints common to a particular industry or occupation will be dispersed. Should they be picked up by primary organisations in the first place, and should they then be passed on, they will be received by the functionaries of numerous different district party committees. As a result, the collective expression of interests common to a particular category of party members meets an organisational barrier and the chances of comprehensive information being assimilated by the party hierarchy and being considered by the decision-making organs is reduced accordingly. The primary party organisation has always remained, therefore, principally an agency through which the party apparatus conveys instructions to the membership, a role which contrasts with the more democratic image set out by the party rules.

In order to increase the capacity of the party to respond to the needs of its rank-and-file members, Medvedev suggested that the lowest echelon of the apparatus, that is at the level of the district party committees, be organised according to the branch rather than the territorial principle. In this way the interests of particular professions, or the views of those employed in the same industry, could be more effectively co-ordinated and would thus be capable of making an impression higher up the party hierarchy than is currently possible. The party might then begin to reflect more adequately the diversity of interests existing among the Soviet population, the structure of which contrasts so clearly with the monolithic organisation of the Soviet state and the inflexible ideology it disseminates.

Today it is difficult to assess with any confidence what the chances of reform may be. Medvedev's suggestions were made on the basis of an analysis of Soviet politics during the 1960s and early 1970s when the situation in the USSR may have seemed more fluid. In the 1980s such ideas may give no more than a helpful insight into the nature of the party's problems; but should reforms be seriously considered by the party leadership Medvedev's suggestions appear to provide the most feasible alternative to persisting centralism.

Science provides an example of an arena in which the costs of maintaining the party's traditional role are likely to become increasingly obvious. In this respect it is almost certainly not alone, for whilst scientists face their own special problems, they share with many others the experience of conflict between professional and political pressures.

Notes and References

1 INTRODUCTION

1. On 1 January 1981 there were 414 048 primary party organisations, 6739, or 1.6 per cent, of which were located in scientific establishments of one kind or another. The total membership of the CPSU at the time of the XXVI Congress in February 1981 was 17 480 768, which included 717 579 candidate members. 'KPSS v tsifrakh', *Partiinaya zhizn'*, no. 14 (1981) pp. 13 and 20.
2. The most conspicuous has been the Nobel Prize winning physicist P. L. Kapitsa: see his *Teoriya, Eksperiment, Praktika* (Moscow: Znanie, 1966) and *Zhizn' dlya nauki, Lomonosov, Franklin, Rezerford, Lanzheven* (Moscow: Znanie, 1965). See also A. N. Nesmeyanov, 'Nauka i proizvodstvo', *Kommunist*, no. 2 (1956) pp. 33–48.
3. As far as the author is aware these points were first discussed by Roy A. Medvedev in *On Socialist Democracy* (London: Macmillan, 1975) p. 121.
4. For a discussion of the domestic critics of the centralisation of the Soviet economy and the political implications of their ideas, see Moshe Lewin, *Political Undercurrents in Soviet Economic Debates* (London: Pluto Press, 1975) particularly ch. 7.
5. See, for example, 'Nauchno-tekhnicheskaya revolyutsiya', in *Filosofskii slovar'* (Moscow: Politizdat, 1972) pp. 268–9.
6. This question is discussed in detail in Chapter 4.
7. See Chapters 4 and 7.

2 SOVIET NATURAL SCIENTISTS

1. *Narodnoe obrazovanie, nauka i kul'tura v SSSR* (Moscow: Statistika, 1977) p. 438: see also E. Zaleski *et al.*, *Science Policy in the USSR* (Paris: OECD, 1969) pp. 542–3 and 545–6.
2. The exact figure was 1 373 300 (*Narodnoe khozyaistvo SSSR v 1980g* (Moscow: Finansy i Statistika, 1981) p. 95).
3. *Vestnik statistiki*, no. 4 (1974) p. 91.
4. Ibid., p. 90.
5. *Osnovnye printsipy i obshchie problemy upravleniya naukoi* (Moscow: Nauka, 1973) pp. 202–3; *Nauchno-tekhnicheskaya revolyutsiya i izmenenie struktury nauchnykh kadrov SSSR* (Moscow: Nauka, 1973) p. 52; V. Krutov, 'Atmosfera poiska', *Izvestiya* (11 January 1972) p. 5.

See also M. N. Rutkevich, 'Sotsiologicheskie issledovaniya problem intelligentsii', *Sotsiologicheskie issledovaniya*, no. 2 (1980) p. 68, and Mervyn Matthews, *Privilege in the Soviet Union* (London: Allen & Unwin, 1978) pp. 117–18.

6. Mark Ya. Azbel, *Refusenik* (London: Hamish Hamilton, 1981) pp. 169–70.

7. *Ustavy Akademii nauk SSSR* (Moscow: Nauka, 1974) para. 2, p. 166.

8. Decree issued by the Central Committee and the USSR Council of Ministers on 3 April 1961, 'O merakh po uluchsheniyu koordinatsii nauchno-issledovatel'skikh rabot v strane i deyatel'nosti Akademii nauk SSSR', *Spravochnik partiinogo rabotnika* (subsequently *SPR*), vyp. 4, pp. 397–403.

9. L. V. Golovanov, 'Sistema upravleniya naukoi v SSSR: voprosy ee sovershenstvovaniya', *Nauchnoe upravlenie obshchestvom*, vyp. 3 (Moscow: Mysl', 1969) p. 42; *Narodnoe khozyaistvo SSSR v 1960g* (Moscow: Gosstatizdat, 1961) p. 787, and *Narodnoe khozyaistvo SSSR v 1961g* (Moscow: Gosstatizdat, 1962) p. 706.

10. Decree issued by the Central Committee and the USSR Council of Ministers on 11 April 1963, 'O merakh po uluchsheniyu deyatel'nosti Akademii nauk SSSR i akademii nauk soyuznykh respublik', *SPR*, vyp. 5, pp. 230–5.

11. *Narodnoe khozyaistvo SSSR v 1962g* (Moscow: Gosstatizdat, 1963) p. 586, and *Narodnoe khozyaistvo SSSR v 1963g* (Moscow: Gosstatizdat, 1964) p. 594; V. I. Duzhenkov, 'Organizatsiya fundamental'nykh issledovanii v akademiyakh nauk soyuznykh respublik', *Organizatsiya nauchnoi deyatel'nosti* (Moscow: Nauka, 1968) pp. 245–6.

12. V. Zh. Kelle, S. A. Kugel' and N. I. Makeshin, 'Sotsiologicheskie aspekty organizatsii truda nauchnykh rabotnikov v sfere fundamental'nykh issledovanii (po materialam konkretno–sotsiologicheskogo issledovaniya)', in *Sotsiologicheskie problemy nauchnoi deyatel'nosti* (Moscow: Institut sotsiologicheskikh issledovanii AN SSSR, 1978) pp. 113 and 121. Somewhat different proportions were given in another piece of research which reported that the majority of scientific workers employed by the USSR Academy of Sciences were engaged in both fundamental and applied research and, to a lesser extent, in development. Only 31 per cent were said to be carrying out fundamental research exclusively. S. A. Kugel' and P. B. Shelishch, 'Nauchnaya intelligentsiya SSSR: faktory i tendentsii razvitiya', *Sotsiologicheskie issledovaniya*, no. 1 (1979) p. 34.

13. *Ustavy Akademii nauk*, para. 1, p. 116.

14. Thane Gustafson, 'Why Doesn't Soviet Science Do Better Than It Does?', in Linda L. Lubrano and Susan Gross Solomon (eds), *The Social Context of Soviet Science* (Folkestone: Wm Dawson, 1980) p. 61.

15. *Narodnoe obrazovanie, nauka i kul'tura v SSSR* (Moscow: Statistika, 1971) pp. 252–3.

16. Ibid.

17. V. Kirillov-Ugryumov, 'Kadry nauki', *Pravda* (29 May 1975) p. 3. .

18. Decree issued by the Central Committee and the USSR Council of Ministers on 18 October 1974, 'O merakh po dal'neishemu sover-

shenstvovaniyu attestatsii nauchnykh i nauchno–pedagogicheskikh kadrov', *SPR*, vyp. 15, pp. 378–82.

19. *Narodnoe obrazovanie* (1971) pp. 252–3; *Kul'turnoe stroitel'stvo SSSR* (Moscow: Gosstatizdat, 1956) p. 250.

20. M. N. Rutkevich, 'Sovetskaya intelligentsiya: struktura i tendentsii razvitiya na sovremennom etape', *Sotsiologicheskie issledovaniya*, no. 2 (1980) pp. 72–3.

21. Medvedev's figures are used because they give a sense of relative pay rates among scientific workers. However, his observations probably relate to the late 1960s or early 1970s, for the average monthly wage for a Soviet industrial worker in 1975 was already 161 roubles and this had risen to 186 by the end of 1980. In science and science services (which includes technicians and other supporting workers) the wage levels for the respective years were 158 and 180 roubles. *Vestnik statistiki*, no. 8 (1981) p. 78; Zhores A. Medvedev, *Soviet Science* (Oxford University Press, 1979) p. 78; Mervyn Matthews, *Privilege in the Soviet Union*, pp. 26–8; see also Murray Yanowitch, *Social and Economic Inequality in the Soviet Union* (London: Martin Robertson, 1977) p. 39; E. Zaleski *et al.*, *Science Policy in the USSR*, p. 411; B. D. Lebin and G. A. Tsypkin, *Prava rabotnika nauki* (Leningrad: Nauka, 1971) p. 139.

22. Zhores A. Medvedev, *Soviet Science*.

23. Mervyn Matthews, *Privilege in the Soviet Union*.

24. Ibid., passim; Hedrick Smith, *The Russians* (London: Times Books, 1976) pp. 38–52.

25. Nicholas De Witt, *Education and Professional Employment in the USSR* (Washington, D. C.: NSF, 1961) p. 418; *Moskva v tsifrakh (1966–1970gg)* (Moscow: Statistika, 1972) p. 138.

26. *Moskva v tsifrakh* (Moscow: Finansy i Statistika, 1981) p. 38; *Narodnoe khozyaistvo SSSR v 1980g* (Moscow: Finansy i Statistika, 1981) p. 97.

27. *Ustavy Akademii nauk*, paras 1–4; *Osnovnye printsipy i obshchie problemy upravleniya naukoi*, p. 180; L. V. Golovanov, in *Nauchnoe upravlenie obshchestvom*, p. 44.

28. *Ustavy Akademii nauk*, paras 169–75; *Vestnik Akademii nauk SSSR*, no. 1 (1976) p. 4.

29. G. P. Kushnarev, 'Razrabotka metodiki konkretno-sotsiologicheskogo issledovaniya nauchnoi deyatel'nosti', in *Sotsiologicheskie problemy nauchnoi deyatel'nosti*, Table 3, p. 94, and *Nauchno-tekhnicheskaya revolyutsiya i izmenenie struktury*, pp. 67 and 113.

30. *Sotsiologicheskie problemy nauchnoi deyatel'nosti,* Table 4, p. 96; *Vestnik statistiki*, no. 4 (1974) p. 91.

3 EDUCATIONAL BACKGROUND AND SOCIAL CHARACTERISTICS

1. V. F. Chernovolenko, V. L. Ossovskii and V. I. Paniotto, *Prestizh professii i problemy sotsial'no-professional'noi orientatsii molodezhi* (Kiev: Naukova Dumka, 1979) pp. 184–5 and 203–6; *Sotsial'no-pro-*

fessional'naya orientatsiya molodezhi (Tartu: Tartuskii Gosudarstvennyi Universitet, 1973) pp. 250–61. Useful description and analysis can also be found in David Lane and Felicity O'Dell, *The Soviet Industrial Worker* (Oxford: Martin Robertson, 1978) pp. 73–7 and Murray Yanowitch and Norton Dodge, 'The Social Evaluation of Occupations in the Soviet Union', *Slavic Review*, vol. 28, no. 1 (March 1969) pp. 619–44.

2. *Nauchno-tekhnicheskaya revolyutsiya i izmenenie struktury nauchnykh kadrov SSSR* (Moscow: Nauka, 1973) p. 52; V. P. Elyutin, 'Za organicheskoe edinstvo nauchnoi i uchebnoi raboty', *Vestnik vysshei shkoly*, no. 9 (1972) pp. 4–6; *Narodnoe obrazovanie, nauka i kul'tura v SSSR* (Moscow: Statistika, 1977) pp. 215–16.

3. Linda L. Lubrano and John K. Berg, 'Scientists in the USA and USSR', *Survey*, vol. 23, no. 1 (Winter 1977–8) pp. 161–93.

4. P. L. Kapitsa, *Teoriya, Eksperiment, Praktika* (Moscow: Znanie, 1966) pp. 35–6.

5. *Bol'shaya Sovetskaya Entsiklopediya* (subsequently *BSE*), 3rd edn, vol. 17 (1974) pp. 37, 45–6; V. Kirillov-Ugryumov, 'Dve stupeni vuza', *Izvestiya* (21 May 1972) p. 3; O. M. Belotserkovskii, 'Sovremennaya nauka i vuzy', *Vestnik Akademii nauk SSSR*, no. 7 (1975) p. 37; V. M. Kolobashkin and V. I. Ivanov, 'Vuzovskaya nauka na styke raznykh oblastei znaniya', *Vestnik Akademii nauk SSSR*, no. 9 (1980) pp. 43–8.

6. Ye. Velikhov and A. Prokhorov, 'Kak gotovit' issledovatelei', *Izvestiya* (25 January 1977) p. 2; see also S. Belyaev, 'Rol' universiteta v podgotovke kadrov dlya nauk', *Vestnik Akademii nauk SSSR*, no. 3 (1976) pp. 31–5; O. M. Belotserkovskii, 'Sovremennaya nauka i vuzy', p. 36–42.

7. Targets for the training of new specialists were set by the plenary sessions of the Communist Party Central Committee of June 1928 and November 1929; see 'Plenum TsK VKP (b), 4–12 iyulya 1928g' and 'Plenum TsK VKP (b), 10–17 noyabrya 1929g', *KPSS v rezolyutsiyakh i resheniyakh s''ezdov, konferentsii i plenumov TsK*, tom 4, 1927–31 (Moscow: Politizdat, 1970) pp. 111–18 and pp. 334–45. Between 1927–8 and 1931–2 the number of students enrolled in Soviet higher educational institutions increased from 159 774 to 394 000 (*Narodnoe khozyaistvo SSSR v 1932g* (Moscow: Sotsekgiz, 1932) p. 507; E. V. Chutkerashvili, *Kadry dlya nauki* (Moscow: Vysshaya shkola, 1968) p. 148; A. E. Beilin, *Kadry spetsialistov SSSR* (Moscow and Leningrad: TsUNKhU Gosplana, 1935) p. 74). For discussion and interpretation of the expansion of the Soviet higher education system see Yu. S. Borisov, 'Izmenenie sotsial'nogo sostava uchashchikhsya vo vysshikh i srednykh spetsial'nykh zavedeniyakh 1917–1940gg', in M. P. Kim (ed.), *Kul'turnaya revolyutsiya v SSSR 1917–1965gg* (Moscow: Nauka, 1967) p. 137, and P. H. Kneen, *Higher Education and Cultural Revolution in the USSR*, Soviet Industrialisation Project, no. 5 (CREES, University of Birmingham, 1976) pp. 41–63.

8. Between 1927–8 and 1931–2 the number of universities operating in the USSR fell from 18 to 11 and the students enrolled in them from 53 000 to 9400, of which 7000 were to be found at the universities of Moscow, Leningrad, Kazan and Rostov. By the end of the decade the enrolment of university students had once more reached nearly 50 000. See E. V.

Chutkerashvili, *Kadry dlya nauki*, pp. 75–80 and P. H. Kneen, *Higher Education*, pp. 45–6 and Table 2, p. 60.

9. P. Khranilov, 'Ostraslevoi ili politekhnicheskii', *Izvestiya* (5 April 1972) p. 3; M. Volkenstein, 'Perekrëstki otkrytii', *Izvestiya* (9 May 1972) p. 5; V. Kirillov-Ugryumov, 'Dve stupeni vuza'.

10. S. T. Belyaev, *Vestnik Akademii nauk SSSR*, pp. 31–5; for a useful summary of inequalities of higher educational opportunity in the USSR see M. Matthews, *Privilege in the Soviet Union* (London: Allen & Unwin, 1978) pp. 114–19.

11. In the 1920s and 1930s workers' faculties (*rabfaki*) were attached to most higher educational institutions in order to increase the proportion of workers among students. They were phased out towards the end of the 1930s as secondary education became more universally available. Since 1969, there has been a return to something approximating to pre-War practice with the setting up of preparatory faculties to serve a similar purpose. *Nauchnye kadry Leningrada* (Leningrad: Nauka, 1973) p. 81; V. Yagodkin, · 'Partiinye organizatsii vuzov i vospitanie molodykh spetsialistov', *Partiinaya zhizn'*, no. 18 (1973) p. 58.

12. A. E. Beilin, *Kadry spetsialistov SSSR*, p. 311.

13. M. N. Rutkevich and F. R. Filippov, *Vysshaya shkola kak faktor izmeneniya sotsial'noi struktury sotsialisticheskogo obshchestva* (Moscow: Nauka, 1978) Table 37, p. 123; see also Ts. A. Stepanyan *et al.* (eds), *Klassy, sotsial'nye sloi i gruppy v SSSR* (Moscow: Nauka, 1968); M. N. Rutkevich and F. R. Filippov, *Sotsial'nye peremeshcheniya* (Moscow: Mysl', 1970); B. Rubin and Yu. Kolesnikov, *Student glazami sotsiologa* (izd. Rostovskogo Universiteta, 1968); M. Matthews, 'Soviet Students – Some Sociological Perspectives', *Soviet Studies*, vol. xxvi, no. 1 (1975) pp. 86–91; M. Yanowitch, *Social and Economic Inequality in the Soviet Union* (London: Martin Robertson, 1977) p. 39.

14. M. N. Rutkevich and F. R. Filippov, *Vysshaya shkola kak faktor*.

15. N. Blinov and N. Sleptsov, 'Sotsiologicheskii portret studentov', *Molodoi Kommunist* (September 1979) pp. 101–2.

16. M. N. Rutkevich and F. R. Filippov, *Vysshaya shkola kak faktor*.

17. Ibid., pp. 137–8; Ts. A. Stepanyan et al, *Klassy, sotsial'nye sloi i gruppy*, pp. 209–12; M. Yanowitch, *Social and Economic Inequality*, pp. 77–91; M. Matthews in *Soviet Studies*, pp. 88–91.

18. M. N. Rutkevich and F. R. Filippov, *Vysshaya shkola kak faktor*, p. 190.

19. *Nauchyne kadry Leningrada*, pp. 79–84.

20. M. N. Rutkevich and F. R. Filippov, *Vysshaya shkola kak faktor*, pp. 248–52.

21. *Vestnik statistiki*, no. 4 (1962) p. 64, and *Vestnik statistiki*, no. 4 (1974) p. 90; *Upravlenie, planirovanie i organizatsiya nauchnykh i tekhnicheskikh issledovanii*, tom 3 (Moscow: VINITI, 1970) pp. 438–9.

22. *Vestnik statistiki*, no. 4 (1974), p. 90.

23. G. P. Kushnarev, 'Razrabotka metodiki konkretno-sotsiologicheskogo issledovaniya nauchnoi deyatel'nosti', in *Sotsiologicheskie problemy nauchnoi deyatel'nosti* (Moscow: Institut sotsiologicheskikh issledovanii AN SSSR, 1978) pp. 95–8.

24. Computed from *Narodnoe obrazovanie, nauka i kul'tura v SSSR* (Moscow: Statistika, 1977) pp. 301 and 307; *Narodnoe khozyaistvo SSSR v 1980g* (Moscow: Finansy i Statistika, 1981) p. 95.
25. Ibid.
26. Kushnarev, in *Sotsiologicheskie problemy nauchnoi deyatel'nosti*, p. 95.
27. Ibid., p. 99.
28. R. G. Butenko, 'Vashe kreslo v Akademii', *Sovetskaya Rossiya* (23 April 1980) p. 4.
29. Ibid.
30. *Narodnoe obrazovanie* (1977) pp. 308, 309, 310.
31. It should be noted that whilst the figures for scientific workers quoted here refer to the end of 1975, those relating to ethnic groups as proportions of the Soviet population refer to the census of 1979. See ibid. and *Narodnoe khozyaistvo SSSR v 1979g* (Moscow: Statistika, 1980) p. 29.
32. N. De Witt, *Education and Professional Employment in the USSR* (Washington, D. C.: NSF, 1961) p. 421.
33. Ibid.; *Narodnoe khozyaistvo SSSR v 1970g* (Moscow: Statistika, 1971) p. 658; *Vestnik statistiki*, no. 4 (1974) p. 92: *Narodnoe obrazovanie* (1977) p. 310.
34. *Vestnik statistiki*, no. 4 (1974) p. 95.
35. G. M. Dobrov, V. N. Klimenyuk, L. P. Smirnov and A. A. Savel'ev, *Potentsial nauki* (Kiev: Naukova Dumka, 1969) p. 52.
36. *Nauchnye kadry Leningrada*, pp. 51–6; see also Table 6.3.
37. Computed from *Vestnik statistiki*, no. 4 (1974) pp. 92–3.

4 SOVIET SCIENTISTS AND WORLD SCIENCE

1. See T. S. Kuhn, *The Structure of Scientific Revolutions* (University of Chicago Press, 1972); T. S. Kuhn, 'The Function of Measurement in Modern Physical Science', in H. Woolf (ed.), *Quantification* (New York: Bobbs-Merrill, 1961) pp. 31–61; M. J. Mulkay, *The Social Process of Innovation* (London and Basingstoke: Macmillan, 1972).
2. On consensus among natural scientists see F. P. Jevons, *The Teaching of Science* (London: Allen & Unwin, 1969) p. 140; T. S. Kuhn, 'Scientific Paradigms', in B. Barnes (ed.), *The Sociology of Science* (Harmondsworth: Penguin Books, 1972) pp. 83–4; M. J. Mulkay, *The Social Process*, pp. 18–30.
3. On the growth of natural science in modern times see Derek de Solla Price, *Little Science, Big Science* (New York: Columbia University Press, 1963) pp. 1–22.
4. Robert K. Merton, 'Singletons and Multiples in Scientific Discovery', *Proceedings of the American Philosophical Society*, cv5 (October 1961) pp. 470–86.
5. Derek de Solla Price, 'Science and Technology: Distinctions and Interrelationships', in B. Barnes (ed.), *The Sociology of Science*, p. 170; M. J. Mulkay, *The Social Process*, pp. 24–5; Robert K. Merton, 'Priorities

in Scientific Discovery', *American Sociological Review*, xxii (1957) pp. 653–59; W. O. Hagstrom, *The Scientific Community* (New York: Basic Books, 1965) pp. 15–16.

6. Derek de Solla Price, 'Science and Technology', pp. 166–80.
7. Ibid., p. 167.
8. Derek de Solla Price, *Little Science, Big Science*, pp. 8–20.
9. V. V. Nalimov and Z. M. Mul'chenko, *Naukometriya* (Moscow: Nauka, 1969); see also Z. B. Barinova *et al.*, 'Izucheniya nauchnykh zhurnalov kak kanalov svyazi', *Nauchno-tekhnicheskaya informatsiya*, seriya 2, no. 12 (1967) pp. 3–11. For an illuminating discussion of the development of *naukovedenie* (science studies) in the Soviet Union see Ya. M. Rabkin, 'The Study of Science', *Survey*, vol. 23, no. 1 (Winter 1977–8) pp. 134–45.
10. The three areas of biology were excluded from the analysis. It was noted that:

> A very special position is occupied by these areas of biology. Here the level of publication is significantly lower than in the other branches of knowledge. The effort expended by other countries on the development of biology is distributed proportionately to their effort in chemistry and physics. It is interesting that a sharp non–correspondence of effort can be observed only in our country.

This seems to be a reference to the consequences of Lysenkoism. V. V. Nalimov and Z. M. Mul'chenko, *Naukometriya*, pp. 146–7.
11. Francis Narin and Mark P. Carpenter, 'National Publications and Citation Comparisons', *Journal of the American Society for Information Science*, vol. 26 (March–April 1975) pp. 80–93.
12. Arthur Holt, 'An Analysis of the Level of Soviet Polymer Research by Means of Citations', Appendix 6B of Ronald Amann, 'The Chemical Industry: Its Level of Modernity and Technological Sophistication', in Ronald Amann, Julian Cooper and R. W. Davies (eds), with the assistance of Hugh Jenkins, *The Technological Level of Soviet Industry* (Newhaven and London: Yale University Press, 1977) pp. 320–8.
13. This ratio was calculated by dividing the percentage of all citations to a given discipline in a given year in a given country by the percentage of the publications in that discipline appearing in that year which originated in the given country. See Francis Narin and Mark P. Carpenter, 'National Publications', p. 89.
14. In addition to the data presented by Narin and Carpenter, see V. V. Nalimov and Z. M. Mul'chenko, *Naukometriya*, p. 146 and Yu. T. Burbulya and V. P. Korbarskaya, 'Issledovanie tsitiruemosti matematicheskoi literatury', *Nauchno-tekhnicheskaya informatsiya*, seriya 2, no. 2 (1978) pp. 10–14.
15. Francis Narin and Mark P. Carpenter, 'National Publications', p. 92.
16. Arthur Holt in R. Amann, J. Cooper and R. W. Davies, *The Technological Level*, p. 325.
17. Zhores A. Medvedev, *The Medvedev Papers* (London: Macmillan, 1971) p. 147.

18. P. L. Kapitsa, *Teoriya, Eksperiment, Praktika* (Moscow: Znanie, 1966) pp. 7–14.

19. Mark Popovsky, 'Science in Blinkers', *Index on Censorship*, vol. 9, no. 4 (August 1980) p. 18; Valentin Turchin, *The Inertia of Fear* (Oxford: Martin Robertson, 1981) p. 84; R. Amann, J. Cooper and R. W. Davies, *The Technological Level*, pp. 290–1.

20. *Nauchno-tekhnicheskaya revolyutsiya i izmenenie struktury nauchnykh kadrov SSSR* (Moscow: Nauka, 1973) pp. 9–26; *Osnovnie printsipy i obshchie problemy upravleniya naukoi* (Moscow: Nauka, 1973) pp. 24–50.

21. V. V. Nalimov and Z. M. Mul'chenko, *Naukometriya*, p. 162.

22. Ibid., pp. 163–7; see also L. L. Balashev, 'Voprosy nauchnoi informatsii v oblasti biologii', *Nauchno-tekhnicheskaya informatsiya*, seriya 2, no. 2 (1967) pp. 9–12, and Arnost Kol'man, 'A Life in Soviet Science Reconsidered: The Adventure of Cybernetics in the Soviet Union', *Minerva*, vol. xvi, no. 3 (Autumn 1978) pp. 416–24.

23. Several studies of informal scientific networks are conveniently discussed and analysed by Diana Crane in 'Transnational Networks in Basic Science', in Robert O. Keohane and Joseph S. Nye Jr (eds), *Transnational Relations and World Politics* (Cambridge, Mass.: Harvard University Press, 1972) pp. 235–51; see also Derek de Solla Price and Donald de B. Beaver, 'Collaboration in an Invisible College', *American Psychologist*, vol. 21 (1966) pp. 1011–18; Nicholas C. Mullins, 'The Development of a Scientific Specialty: The Phage Group and the Origins of Molecular Biology', *Minerva*, vol. 10, no. 1 (1972) pp. 51–82; John Ziman, 'Soviet Science and the Invisible College', *The Listener* (10 June 1976) pp. 725–726. On the paucity of international co-authorships involving Soviet scientists, see J. Davidson-Frame and Mark P. Carpenter, 'International Research Collaboration', *Social Studies of Science*, vol. 9, no. 4 (November 1979) p. 490.

24. For analysis of participants in international exchange programmes see Earl Callen, 'US-Soviet Scientific Exchange in the Age of Detente', *Survey*, vol. 21, no. 4 (Autumn 1975) pp. 52–9, and Robert F. Byrnes, 'Soviet-American Academic Exchange', *Survey*, vol. 22, no. 3–4 (Summer–Autumn 1976) pp. 26–38.

25. Arnost Kol'man observes:

> Delegations to international scientific congresses have to be approved by the Central Committee of the Communist Party and as a result they consist not of genuine scientists, but of administrators who are not able to take part in the discussion of scientific problems; in all such delegations there is an informer who is assigned to it by the KGB.

See 'A Life in Soviet Science Reconsidered', pp. 416–24; see also Zhores A. Medvedev, *The Medvedev Papers*, pp. 19–20; J. D. Nye, 'Russians at Conferences' (correspondence), *Nature*, vol. 249 (3 May 1974) p. 8, and Philip H. Abelson, 'International Geophysics: Science Dominates Politics', *Science*, 190 (3 October 1975) p. 34.

26. See, for example, J. Gaston, 'Communication and the Reward System of Science: A Study of a National "Invisible College"', *Sociological Review Monograph*, 18, pp. 25–41.

27. V. V. Nalimov and Z. M. Mul'chenko, *Naukometriya*, pp. 163–4.

28. M. J. Mulkay, *The Social Process*, pp. 35–6.

29. V. V. Nalimov and Z. M. Mul'chenko, *Naukometriya*, pp. 184–6.

30. Thane Gustafson, 'Why Doesn't Soviet Science Do Better Than It Does?', in Linda L. Lubrano and Susan Gross Solomon (eds), *The Social Context of Soviet Science* (Folkestone: Wm Dawson, 1980) p. 35.

31. M. J. Mulkay, *The Social Process*, p. 22; William R. Shelton, 'Science in Siberia', *Bulletin of the Atomic Scientists* (February 1971) pp. 23–8.

32. Zhores A. Medvedev, *The Medvedev Papers*, pp. 7–45.

33. B. P. Gottikh and G. G. Dyumenton, 'Lichnye nauchnye kommunikatsii i organizatsiya fundamental'nykh issledovanii', *Vestnik Akademii nauk SSSR*, vol. 12 (1979) pp. 65–78.

34. Ibid., p. 77.

35. Ibid., p. 68.

36. At the end of 1970, 25.2 per cent of Soviet scientific workers were employed in Moscow (*Moskva v tsifrakh* (*1966–1970gg*) (Moscow: Statistika, 1972) p. 138).

37. K. B. Serebrovskaya, 'Sovremennyi neformal'nyi kollektiv v fundamental'nykh issledovaniyakh', in *Sotsial'no-psikhologicheskie problemy nauki* (Moscow: Nauka, 1973) pp. 96–127.

38. On this and other points see Linda L. Lubrano 'Scientific Collectives: Behaviour of Soviet Scientists in Basic Research', in L. L. Lubrano and S. G. Solomon, *The Social Context*, pp. 101–36; see also V. Zh. Kelle et al. in *Sotsiologicheskie problemy nauchnoi deyatel'nosti* (Moscow: Institut sotsiologicheskikh issledovanii AN SSSR, 1978) Table 8, p. 129, for survey data on the relative importance to natural scientists in the academies of sciences of informal relations inside and outside the institute in which they are employed.

39. L. L. Lubrano, in L. L. Lubrano and S. G. Solomon, *The Social Context*, p. 117.

40. R. Amann, in R. Amann, J. Cooper and R. W. Davies, *The Technological Level*, p. 294.

41. On the comparative slowness of Soviet scientific journals, see Yu. B. Granovskii, *Naukometricheskii analiz informatsionnykh potokov v khimii* (Moscow: Nauka, 1980) pp. 64–7; L. L. Balashev, *Nauchno-tekhnicheskaya informatsiya*, pp. 9–12; A. Kol'man, 'A Life in Soviet Science Reconsidered; V. V. Nalimov and Z. M. Mul'chenko, *Naukometriya*, pp. 153–5; Zhores A. Medvedev, *Soviet Science* (Oxford and Melbourne: Oxford University Press, 1979) pp. 153–7.

42. R. Amann, in R. Amann, J. Cooper and R. W. Davies, *The Technological Level*, pp. 293–4.

43. Ibid.

44. V. V. Nalimov and Z. M. Mul'chenko, *Naukometriya*, pp. 151–3.

45. R. Kaiser, *Russia: The People and the Power* (Harmondsworth: Penguin Books, 1977) pp. 275–95; Zhores A. Medvedev, *The Medvedev Papers*, pp. 165–7.

46. T. Gustafson, in L. L. Lubrano and S. G. Solomon, *The Social Context*, p. 54; see also V. Zh. Kelle *et al.* in *Sotsiologicheskie problemy nauchnoi deyatel'nosti*, Table 6, p. 127, which shows that 63 per cent of sampled Soviet natural scientists were not satisfied with the material-technical supply system.

47. For further comment relevant to this point, see Gustafson in L. L. Lubrano and S. G. Solomon, *The Social Context*, pp. 46–7.

48. Mark Ya. Azbel, *Refusenik* (London: Hamish Hamilton, 1981) pp. 335–6.

5 PLANNING AND LEADERSHIP

1. *Ustavy Akademii nauk SSSR, 1724–1974gg* (Moscow: Nauka, 1974) pp. 166–7; for discussion of the role of the USSR Academy of Sciences see *Osnovnye printsipy i obshchie problemy upravleniya naukoi* (Moscow: Nauka, 1973) p. 180; V. A. Rassudovskii, *Gosudarstvennaya organizatsiya nauki v SSSR* (Moscow: Yuridicheskaya Literature, 1971) pp. 32–49; L. V. Golovanov, 'Sistema upravleniya naukoi v SSSR i voprosy ee sovershenstvovaniya', in *Nauchnoe upravlenie obshchestvom*, vyp. 3 (Moscow: Mysl', 1969) p. 44; *Organizatsionno-pravovye voprosy rukovodstva naukoi v SSSR* (Moscow: Nauka, 1973) pp. 208–9.

2. *Ustavy Akademii nauk SSSR* (1974) pp. 175–6 and 178–9; K. A. Lange, *Organizatsiya upravleniya nauchnymi issledovaniyami* (Leningrad: Nauka, 1971) pp. 168–88; *Osnovnye printsipy*, pp. 189–91.

3. *Organizatsionno-pravovye voprosy rukovodstva naukoi v SSSR*, pp. 269–86; *Nauchno-tekhnicheskaya revolyutsiya i izmenenie struktury nauchnykh kadrov SSSR* (Moscow: Nauka, 1973) pp. 42–3.

4. Ibid.; see also *Nauchnye kadry Leningrada* (Leningrad: Nauka, 1973) pp. 92–3.

5. The framework within which science has been planned in recent years was set out in the decree, 'O meropriyatiyakh po povysheniyu effektivnosti raboty nauchnykh organizatsii i uskoreniya ispol'zovaniya v narodnom khozyaistve dostizhenii nauki i tekhniki', issued by the Central Committee and the USSR Council of Ministers on 24 September 1968, *SPR*, vyp. 9, pp. 257–83.

6. V. A. Kirillin, *Vestnik Akademii nauk SSSR*, no. 5 (1976) p. 48; *Osnovnye printsipy*, p. 46; see also Loren R. Graham, 'The Role of the Academy of Sciences', *Survey*, vol. 23, no. 1, (Winter 1977–8) p. 119.

7. V. A. Kirillin, 'Ob uchastii profsoyuzov v osushchestvlennii tekhnicheskogo progressa v narodnom khozyaistve', *Trud* (2 October 1968) p. 2.

8. *Osnovnye printsipy*, pp. 192–6; see also Yu. Sheinin, *Science Policy: Problems and Trends* (Moscow: Progress Publishers, 1978) p. 203.

9. V. A. Kirillin, *Vestnik Akademii nauk SSSR*; V. Prokrovskii, 'Upravlenie effektivnost'yu nauki i tekhniki', *Ekonomicheskaya gazeta*, no. 32 (August 1977) p. 10.

10. Ibid.

11. V. L. Tal'roze and S. A. Tsyganov, 'Vozmozhnosti ispol'zovaniya programmo-tselevykh metodov pri planirovanii fundamental'nykh issledovanii na urovne nauchnogo uchrezdeniya', *Vestnik Akademii nauk SSSR*, no. 1 (1981) pp. 57–61; L. Yu. Gervitz and V. V. Rozanov, 'Analiz opyta, problem i perspektiv primeneniya programmo-tselevykh metodov v sisteme AN SSSR', *Vestnik Akademii nauk SSSR*, no. 1 (1981) pp. 77–81.
12. John Löwenhardt, 'Scientist-entrepreneurs in the Soviet Union', *Survey*, vol. 20, no. 4 (Autumn 1974) pp. 116–17.
13. *Osnovnye printsipy*, p. 197.
14. V. L. Tal'roze and S. A. Tsyganov, 'Vozmozhnosti ispol'zovaniya', p. 58.
15. G. M. Dobrov, V. N. Klimenyuk, V. M. Odrin and A. A. Savel'ev, *Organizatsiya nauki* (Kiev: Naukova Dumka, 1970) pp. 62–4; I. V. Sergeeva, 'Kollektiv i lichnost' v nauke', *Sotsial'nye issledovaniya*, vyp. 3 (Moscow: Nauka, 1970) p. 185; I. I. Leiman, *Nauka kak sotsial'nyi institut* (Leningrad: Nauka, 1971) pp. 163–72.
16. *Effektivnost' nauchnykh issledovanii* (Alma-Ata: Nauka KSSR, 1978) p. 247.
17. I. V. Sergeeva, in *Sotsial'nye issledovaniya*, p. 185.
18. G. M. Dobrov, V. N. Klimenyuk *et al.*, *Organizatsiya nauki*, p. 86; *Effektivnost' nauchnykh issledovanii*, p. 241; Thane Gustafson, 'Why Doesn't Soviet Science Do Better Than It Does?', in Linda L. Lubrano and Susan Gross Solomon (eds), *The Social Context of Soviet Science* (Folkestone: Wm Dawson, 1980) pp. 48–54; Zhores A. Medvedev, *The Medvedev Papers* (London: Macmillan, 1971) pp. 165–7. For comment on the operation of the material-technical supply system and the political significance of maintaining its centralised structure, see Moshe Lewin, *Political Undercurrents in Soviet Economic Debates* (London: Pluto Press, 1975) p. 280; Hedrick Smith, *The Russians* (London: Times Books, 1976) pp. 227–8 and Robert Kaiser, *Russia: The People and the Power* (Harmondsworth: Penguin Books, 1977) pp. 304–6.
19. A. V. Rzhanov, 'O nekotorykh putyakh povysheniya effektivnosti fundamental'nykh nauchnykh issledovanii', *Vestnik Akademii nauk SSSR*, no. 2 (1982) pp. 41–7. On the material-technical supply system as a cause of dissatisfaction among scientists see V. Zh. Kelle *et al.* in *Sotsiologicheskie problemy nauchnoi deyatel'nosti* (Moscow: Institut sotsiologicheskikh issledovanii AN SSSR, 1978) Table 6, p. 127; see also G. M. Dobrov, V. N. Klimenyuk *et al.*, *Organizatsiya nauki*, pp. 47, 67–9 and 86–7; B. A. Frolov, 'Motivatsiya tvorchestva v nauchnom kollective', in *Sotsial'no-psikhologicheskie problemy nauki* (Moscow: Nauka, 1973) p. 150; V. Semenov, 'Fond dlya nauki', *Pravda* (27 December 1968) p. 2; I. I. Leiman, *Nauka kak sotsial'nyi institut*, p. 142.
20. K. A. Lange, *Organizatsiya upravleniya nauchnymi issledovaniyami*, pp. 216–17.
21. V. Zh. Kelle *et al.* in *Sotsiologicheskie problemy nauchnoi deyatel'nosti*, Table 6, p. 127; see also B. A. Frolov, in *Sotsial'no-psikhologicheskie problemy nauki*, pp. 147–52; V. V. Poshataev, 'Nauchnyi kollektiv kak sfera formirovaniya individual'nosti', in *Nauchnoe upravlenie*

obshchestvom, vyp. 5 (Moscow: Mysl', 1971) pp. 201–2; Thane Gustafson, in L. L. Lubrano and S. G. Solomon, *The Social Context*, pp. 46–7.

22. V. Zh. Kelle *et al.*, *Sotsiologicheskie problemy nauchnoi deyatel'nosti*, pp. 130–3.

23. B. A. Frolov, in *Sotsial'no-psikhologicheskie problemy nauki*, pp. 150–1; Thane Gustafson, in L. L. Lubrano and S. G. Solomon, *The Social Context*, p. 47.

24. V. V. Poshataev, in *Nauchnoe upravlenie obshchestvom*, pp. 216–17; I. I. Leiman, *Nauka kak sotsial'nyi institut*, pp. 138–42; see also Linda L. Lubrano, 'Scientific Collectives: Behaviour of Soviet Scientists in Basic Research', in L. L. Lubrano and S. G. Solomon, *The Social Context*, pp. 124–9.

25. I.V. Sergeeva, in *Sotsial'nye issledovaniya*, p. 188.

26. Ibid., p. 188; V. V. Poshataev, *Nauchnoe upravlenie obshchestvom*, p. 212. *Nauchno-tekhnicheskaya revolyutsiya i izmenenie struktury nauchnykh kadrov SSSR*, pp. 43–4.

27. *Nauchnye kadry Leningrada*, pp. 106–12.

28. Ibid., pp. 111–12.

29. Ibid.

30. *Sotsial'no-psikhologicheskie problemy nauki*, p. 150; S. A. Kugel', 'Struktura i dinamika nauchnykh kadrov', in *Upravlenie, planirovanie i organizatsiya nauchnykh i tekhnicheskikh issledovanii*, tom 2 (Moscow: VINITI, 1971) p. 236.

31. P. L. Kapitsa, *Teoriya, Eksperiment, Praktika* (Moscow: Znanie, 1966) pp. 4–5.

32. Ibid., p. 18.

33. *Nauchno-tekhnicheskaya revolyutsiya i izmenenie struktury nauchnykh kadrov SSSR*, p. 43; see also V. Zh. Kelle *et al.* in *Sotsiologicheskie problemy nauchnoi deyatel'nosti*, p. 119 and Table 6, p. 127.

34. Ibid., Table 26, p. 141.

6 NATURAL SCIENTISTS AND THE COMMUNIST PARTY

1. 'KPSS v tsifrakh', *Partiinaya zhizn'*, no. 14 (1981), p. 20.

2. *Rules of the CPSU* (Moscow: Progress Publishers, 1977) pp. 34–42.

3. Yu. Burlin, 'Partorganizatsiya i effektivnost' vuzovskoi nauki', *Partiinaya zhizn'*, no. 20 (1976) p. 32.

4. 'KPSS v tsifrakh', p. 21.

5. Yu. Burlin, 'Partorganizatsiya', p. 32; Ronald J. Hill and Peter Frank, *The Soviet Communist Party* (London: George Allen & Unwin, 1981) pp. 22–3 and 51. Whereas the party committees of rural districts (*raikoms*) are directly subordinated to their respective regional party committees (*obkoms*), larger cities are subdivided into urban districts, which introduces an extra tier into the party hierarchy in the form of the city party committee (*gorkom*). The city party committees of Moscow and Kiev, however, have been granted the status of regional committees.

6. *Rules of the CPSU*, pp. 18–34.

7. Jerry F. Hough and Merle Fainsod, *How the Soviet Union is Governed* (Cambridge, Mass., and London: Harvard University Press, 1979) pp. 456–7; Boris Meissner, 'The 26th Congress and Soviet Domestic Politics', *Problems of Communism* (May–June 1981) pp. 1–23.

8. R. J. Hill and P. Frank, *The Soviet Communist Party*, p. 60.

9. Ibid., p. 62.

10. Ibid., pp. 59–62; J. F. Hough and M. Fainsod, *How the Soviet Union is Governed*, pp. 411 and 493; B. Meissner, *Problems of Communism*, p. 9.

11. J. F. Hough and M. Fainsod, *How the Soviet Union is Governed*, pp. 412–17; *BSE*, 3rd edn, vol. 12 (Moscow: Sovetskaya Entsiklopediya, 1973) p. 561. For the purposes of this study the organisation of the party apparatus at the level of the central committees of the union republics may be regarded as sufficiently similar to that of the regional party committees to require no separate treatment.

12. M. Tatu, *Power in the Kremlin* (London: Collins, 1969) p. 292; Merle Fainsod, *How Russia is Ruled* (Cambridge, Mass.: Harvard University Press, 1967) pp. 193–202; Loren R. Graham, *Science and Philosophy in the Soviet Union* (London: Allen Lane, 1971) pp. 444–9; J. F. Hough and M. Fainsod, *How the Soviet Union is Governed*, pp. 411, 425 and 644.

13. See, for example, R. G. Yanovskii, *Politicheskaya ucheba v nauchnom kollektive* (Moscow: Politizdat, 1974).

14. V. Yagodkin, 'Partiinye organizatsii vuzov i vospitanie molodykh spetsialistov', *Partiinaya zhizn'*, no. 18 (1973) p. 64.

15. A Shumakov, 'Nauchnym issledovaniyam – vysokuyu effektivnost'', *Partiinaya zhizn'*, no. 2 (1974) pp. 29–30.

16. J. F. Hough and M. Fainsod, *How the Soviet Union is Governed*, p. 495.

17. *XVIII s"ezd VKP (b): Stenograficheskii otchët* (Moscow: Politizdat, 1939) pp. 571–2; see also L. Schapiro, *The Communist Party of the Soviet Union* (London: Methuen, 1970) p. 454.

18. Roy A. Medvedev, *On Socialist Democracy* (London: Macmillan, 1975) p. 117. The correct titles of the government agencies to which Medvedev refers are: the USSR Ministry of Higher and Secondary Specialised Education, and the USSR State Committee for Science and Technology.

19. See J. F. Hough and M. Fainsod, *How the Soviet Union is Governed*, pp. 410–24. Here it is estimated that the Central Committee apparatus employs about 1500 responsible officials. See also A. Avtorkhanov, *The Communist Party Apparatus* (Cleveland and New York: Meridian, 1966) pp. 209–10; A. Pravdin, 'Inside the CPSU Central Committee' (interview with Mervyn Matthews), *Survey*, vol. 20, no. 4 (Autumn 1974) pp. 94–104; L. Schapiro, 'The General Department of the CC of the CPSU', *Survey*, vol. 21, no. 3 (Summer 1975) pp. 53–65.

20. For relevant commentary, see J. F. Hough and M. Fainsod, *How the Soviet Union is Governed*, p. 410 and pp. 476–7, and M. Fainsod, *How Russia is Ruled*, p. 282.

21. *XXIV s"ezd KPSS: Stenograficheskii otchët*, vol. 1 (Moscow: Politizdat, 1971) p. 122; 'Chastichnye izmeneniya v ustave KPSS, vnesennye XXIV s"ezdom KPSS', *Partiinaya zhizn'*, no. 9 (1971) p. 12.

22. M. Alferov, 'Ideinaya zakalka nauchnykh kadrov', *Partiinaya zhizn'*, no. 15 (1972) p. 55.

23. Yu. V. Sachkov and V. P. Chekurin, 'Filosofskie (metodologicheskie) seminary v nauchnykh uchrezhdeniyakh', *Vestnik Akademii nauk SSSR*, no. 4 (1980) p. 46.
24. V. Polunin, 'Raikom i nauchnye kollektivy', *Kommunist*, no. 9 (1980) p. 40.
25. Yu. V. Sachkov and V. P. Chekurin, 'Filosofskie', pp. 42 and 47.
26. M. Alferov, *Partiinaya zhizn'*; R. G. Yanovskii, *Politicheskaya ucheba v nauchnom kollektive*, p. 19.
27. Yu. A. Ovchinnikov, 'Zadacha filosofskikh (metodologicheskikh) seminarov', *Vestnik Akademii nauk SSSR*, no. 2 (1982) pp. 49–56.
28. M. N. Rutkevich, 'Ideino-teoreticheskaya podgotovka nauchnykh kadrov', *Partiinaya zhizn'*, no. 10 (1976) pp. 24–9; V. Yagodkin, 'Partiinaya zhizn' v nauchnykh kollektivakh', *Kommunist*, no. 11 (1972) pp. 59–60; Yu. V. Sachkov and V. P. Chekurin, 'Filosofskie', p. 53.
29. B. Harasymiw, '*Nomenklatura*: The Soviet Communist Party's Leadership Recruitment System', *Canadian Journal of Political Science*, vol. 2, no. 4 (December 1969) p. 503. For useful comment on the *nomenklatura* system see B. D. Lebin and M. N. Perfil'ev, *Kadry apparata upravleniya v SSSR* (Leningrad: Nauka, 1971) pp. 156–9.
30. Yu. P. Sviridenko, 'Sovershenstvovat' partiinoe rukovodstvo kafedrami', *Vestnik vysshei shkoly*, no. 12 (1980) p. 57.
31. Yu. Burlin, 'Partorganizatiya', p. 36; V. Sergeev, 'Partiinaya organizatsiya nauchnogo uchrezhdeniya', *Kommunist*, no. 6 (1972) p. 100.
32. V. Yagodkin, 'Partiinaya zhizn'' (1972); R. L. Dubov, 'Podvedenie itogov sotsialisticheskogo sorevnovaniya v akademicheskikh institutakh', *Vestnik Akademii nauk SSSR*, no. 4 (1980) pp. 106–8.
33. This is discussed in more detail in Chapter 7.
34. T. H. Rigby, *Communist Party Membership in the USSR 1917–67* (Princeton University Press, 1968) pp. 449–51. See also J. F. Hough and M. Fainsod, *How the Soviet Union is Governed*, pp. 347–51.
35. In 1975–6 53 per cent of scientific workers with higher degrees were members of the party, which represents an increase of 3 per cent over the incidence recorded during the previous decade and a half. See Table 6.1.
36. T. H. Rigby, *Communist Party Membership*, p. 450.
37. Ibid., pp. 443–7.
38. *Podgotovka kadrov v SSSR 1927–31gg* (Moscow-Leningrad: Sotsekgiz, 1933) p. 47.
39. T. H. Rigby, *Communist Party Membership*, p. 443.
40. Ibid., p. 446–7; *Kul'turnoe stroitel'stvo SSSR* (Moscow: Gosstatizdat, 1956) p. 248; 'KPSS v tsifrakh', *Partiinaya zhizn'*, no. 1 (1962) p. 48.
41. A. Vucinich, *The Soviet Academy of Sciences* (Stanford University Press, 1956) p. 38.
42. J. F. Hough and M. Fainsod, *How the Soviet Union is Governed*, p. 348.
43. G. D. Komkov, O. M. Karpenko, B. V. Levshin and L. K. Semenov, *Akademiya nauk shtab sovetskoi nauki* (Moscow: Nauka, 1968) p. 185; J. F. Hough and M. Fainsod, *How the Soviet Union is Governed*, p. 348.
44. 'KPSS v tsifrakh', *Partiinaya zhizn'*, no. 1 (1962) p. 48.

45. Rigby estimated that by 1964 scientific workers would account for 2.5 per cent of all party members. This assumed 50 per cent saturation of scientific workers, both with and without higher degrees, among whom the level had been increasing in the post-war years. In 1947 37 per cent of scientific workers were members of the party, rising to 40 per cent in 1950 and 43 per cent in 1955–6, since when figures appear not to have been released. See T. H. Rigby, *Communist Party Membership*, pp. 446–8; *Kul'turnoe stroitel'stvo SSSR*, p. 248; 'KPSS v tsifrakh', *Partiinaya zhizn'*, no. 1 (1962) p. 48.

46. At the end of 1954 there were 210 200 scientific workers, of whom 78 000 had higher degrees. By the end of 1969 there were 883 000, of whom 227 600 had higher degrees. *Narodnoe obrazovanie nauka i kul'tura v SSSR* (Moscow: Statistika, 1971) p. 246.

47. At the end of 1980 there were nearly 1 400 000 scientific workers. If half of them were party members this would equal over 4 per cent of the almost 17½ million membership recorded at the XXVI Party Congress in February 1981. *Narodnoe khozyaistvo SSSR v 1980g* (Moscow: Finansy i Statistika, 1981) pp. 96–7; 'KPSS v tsifrakh', *Partiinaya zhizn'*, no. 14 (1981) p. 13. It may be noted that this issue of *Partiinaya zhizn'* states that on 1 January 1981 4.4 per cent of party members were employed in 'science' (p. 19). It should be pointed out that this category is not synonymous with that of 'scientific worker' as defined by the USSR Central Statistical Administration (see Chapter 2) and as used throughout this study. The *Partiinaya zhizn'* definition excludes those employed in higher educational institutions from 'science', whereas the USSR Central Statistical Administration includes the teaching staffs of such establishments in its definition of a 'scientific worker'. The *Partiinaya zhizn'* definition probably substantially overlaps with that which denotes the 'sphere of science'. This is a much broader category than 'scientific worker' and includes technical and other supporting staff employed in the research and development system as well as scientists and scholars.

48. *Moskovskaya gorodskaya i moskovskaya oblastnaya organizatsii KPSS v tsifrakh* (Moscow: Moskovskii rabochii, 1972) pp. 68–72.

49. *Moskva v tsifrakh (1966–1970 gg)* (Moscow: Statistika, 1972) p. 138.

50. See *Kul'turnoe stroitel'stvo SSSR*, p. 248; 'KPSS v tsifrakh', *Partiinaya zhizn'*, no. 1 (1962) p. 48.

51. O. Yu. Shmidt, 'Problema nauchnykh kadrov', *Vestnik Kommunisticheskoi Akademii*, kniga 37–8 (1930) p. 17.

52. T. H. Rigby, *Communist Party Membership*, p. 444–5.

53. E. V. Chutkerashvili, *Kadry dlya nauki* (Moscow: Vysshaya shkola, 1968) p. 310.

54. V. P. Elyutin, 'Vysshaya shkola v svete reshenii XXIV s''ezda KPSS', *Partiinaya zhizn'*, no. 7 (1973) p. 14; J. F. Hough and M. Fainsod, *How the Soviet Union is Governed*, p. 349.

55. G. D. Komkov, B. V. Levshin and E. K. Semenov, *Akademiya nauk SSSR* (Moscow: Nauka, 1974) p. 462.

56. *Nauchnye kadry Leningrada* (Leningrad: Nauka, 1973) p. 54.

57. Ibid., p. 54.

58. J. F. Hough and M. Fainsod, *How the Soviet Union is Governed*, pp. 347–8.

59. *Nauchnye kadry Leningrada*, p. 55.
60. *Narodnoe khozyaistvo SSSR v 1973g* (Moscow: Statistika, 1974) p. 176.
61. J. F. Hough and M. Fainsod, *How the Soviet Union is Governed*, p. 348.
62. *BSE*, 3rd edn, vol. 1 (Moscow: Sovetskaya Entsiklopediya, 1970) p. 412.
63. See Table 6.1.

7 COMMUNIST PARTY POLICY TOWARDS NATURAL SCIENTISTS

1. The rapid increase in the number of scientific workers during the 1960s is described in detail in Chapter 2.
2. Decree issued by the Central Committee on 29 September 1965, 'Ob uluchshenii upravleniya promyshlennost'yu sovershenstvovanii planirovaniya i usilenii ekonomicheskogo stimulirovaniya promyshlennogo proizvodstva', *SPR*, vyp. 6, p. 112. For a useful discussion of the political implications of the economic changes under consideration at this time, see M. Lewin, *Political Undercurrents in Soviet Economic Debates* (London: Pluto Press, 1975).
3. *Nauchno-tekhnicheskaya revolyutsiya i izmenenie struktury nauchnykh kadrov SSSR* (Moscow: Nauka, 1973) p. 11.
4. Ibid., p. 61.
5. For the slowdown in the expansion of scientific manpower, see Chapter 2. The framework for scientific and technical policy was defined by a decree issued jointly by the Central Committee and the USSR Council of Ministers on 24 September 1968, 'O meropriyatiyakh po povysheniyu effektivnosti raboty nauchnykh organizatsii i uskoreniyu ispol'zovaniya v narodnom khozyaistve dostizhenii nauki i tekhniki', *SPR*, vyp. 9, pp. 257–83.
6. V. Yagodkin, 'Partiinaya zhizn' v nauchnykh kollektivakh', *Kommunist*, no. 11 (1972) pp. 51–2.
7. Ibid.; B. Chaplin, 'Raionnyi komitet partii i nauchno-tekhnicheskaya intelligentsiya', *Kommunist*, no. 7 (1974) p. 48.
8. O. Yamolovich, 'Ideinaya zakalka nauchno-tekhnicheskoi intelligentsii', *Partiinaya zhizn'*, no. 16 (1970) p. 54.
9. B. Chaplin, 'Raionnyi komitet partii', p. 47.
10. Ibid.; V. Yagodkin, *Kommunist*, p. 59; see also *Nauchnye kadry Leningrada* (Leningrad: Nauka, 1973) p. 140.
11. These decisions were contained in two decrees published jointly by the Central Committee and the USSR Council of Ministers in April 1961 and April 1963. See Chapter 2 for details.
12. Zhores Medvedev, *The Rise and Fall of T. D. Lysenko* (New York: Columbia University Press, 1969) pp. 197–220, and 'Two Decades of Dissidence', *New Scientist*, vol. 72 (1976) pp. 264–7; Mark Adams, 'Biology after Stalin: A Case Study', *Survey*, vol. 23, no. 1 (Winter 1977–8) pp. 53–80; David Joravsky, *The Lysenko Affair* (Cambridge, Mass.: Harvard University Press, 1971) pp. 157–86.
13. A. D. Sakharov, *Sakharov Speaks* (London: Collins & Harvill, 1974) pp. 32–4.

14. For illuminating comments see Zhores Medvedev, *The Medvedev Papers* (London: Macmillan, 1971) pp. 283-93.

15. See the decree of the Central Committee and the USSR Council of Ministers issued on 24 September 1968 (note 5 above).

16. Decree issued by the Central Committee on 25 September 1970, 'O rabote partiinogo komiteta fizicheskogo instituta imeni P. N. Lebedeva Akademii nauk SSSR', *SPR*, vyp. 11, pp. 275-8.

17. A. D. Sakharov, *Progress, Coexistence and Intellectual Freedom* (Harmondsworth: Penguin Books, 1969). For details of the circumstances in which Sakharov came to be re-employed by the Lebedev Physics Institute, see Harrison Salisbury's forward to A. D. Sakharov, *Sakharov Speaks*, p. 17.

18. V. Kozhemako, 'Potentsial prakticheski bezgranichen...', *Pravda* (2 December 1970) p. 2.

19. *XXIV s''ezd KPSS: Stenograficheskii otchët*, tom 1 (Moscow: Politizdat, 1971) p. 122; *Partiinaya zhizn'*, no. 9 (1971) p. 12.

20. An editorial in Pravda criticised some theatres and studios in Moscow, referring to 'ideologically immature works and attempts to misrepresent the ideological and artistic meaning of the classics in the guise of a "new reading"'. See 'Neprimirimost' k burzhuaznoi ideologii', *Pravda* (23 November 1970). Social scientists were also criticised in the early 1970s. See the decree published by the Central Committee in January, 1972, 'O rabote partiinoi organizatsii Instituta ekonomiki Akademii nauk SSSR po vypolneniyu postanovleniya TsK KPSS, O merakh po dal'neishemu razvitiyu obshchestvennykh nauk i povysheniya ikh roli v kommunisticheskom stroitel'stve', *Kommunist*, no. 1 (1972) pp. 3-5. Since this chapter was completed an informative article has been published on the right of party control in research establishments: see Stephen Fortescue, 'Research Institute Party Organisations and the Right of Control', *Soviet Studies*, vol. xxxv, no. 2 (April 1983) pp. 175-95.

21. Decree issued jointly by the Central Committee and the USSR Council of Ministers on 18 July 1972, 'O merakh po dal'neishemy sovershenstvovaniyu vysshego obrazovaniya v strane', *SPR*, vyp. 13, pp. 202-10.

22. Decree issued by the Central Committee on 10 July 1973, 'O khode vypolneniya partiinogo organizatsii Leningradskogo politekhnicheskogo instituta imeni M. I. Kalinina reshenii TsK KPSS po povysheniyu urovnya uchebno-vospitatel'noi i nauchnoi raboty', *SPR*, vyp. 14, pp. 333-6.

23. V. Yagodkin, 'Partiinye organizatsii vuzov i vospitanie molodykh spetsialistov', *Partiinaya zhizn'*, no. 18 (1973) p. 62.

24. Decree issued by the Central Committee on 5 June 1974, 'O rabote v Moskovskom vysshem tekhnicheskom uchilishche imeni N. E. Baumana i Saratovskom Gosudarstvennom Universitete imeni N. G. Chernishevskogo po povysheniyu ideino-teoreticheskogo urovnya prepodavaniya obshchestvennykh nauk', *SPR*, vyp. 15, pp. 356-61.

25. S. A. Kugel' and O. M. Nikandrov, *Molodye inzhenery* (Moscow: Mysl', 1971) pp. 105-6; S. F. Esareva, *Osobennosti deyatel'nosti prepodavatelya vysshei shkoly* (Leningrad: izd. LGU, 1974) p. 29. For useful commentary

see M. Matthews, 'Soviet Students – Some Sociological Perspectives', *Soviet Studies*, vol. xxvi, no. 1 (Jaunary 1975) pp. 86–108.

26. R. Yanovskii, 'Ideinost' uchenogo', *Sovetskaya Rossiya* (28 August 1970) p. 2; 'Partiinyi kontrol' v vuze', *Partiinaya zhizn'*, no. 6 (1973) p. 33; V. Yagodkin, *Partiinaya zhizn'*, p. 61.

27. *SPR*, vyp. 15, pp. 357–8.

28. Decree issued jointly by the Central Committee and the USSR Council of Ministers on 18 October 1974, 'O merakh po dal'neishemu sovershenstvovaniyu attestatsii nauchnykh i nauchno-pedagogicheskikh kadrov', *SPR*, vyp. 15, pp. 378–82.

29. N. Vladimirov and I. Afanas'ev, 'Uchenye i lzheuchenye', *Literaturnaya gazeta* (5 June 1974) p. 11, and continued (11 June 1974) p. 12. For useful comment on this decree see Zhores Medvedev, *Soviet Science* (Oxford University Press, 1979) pp. 178–80, and Mark Popovsky, *Science in Chains* (London: Collins & Harvill, 1980) pp. 121–30.

30. See, for example, V. Kirillov-Ugryumov, 'Sistema attestatsii nauchnykh kadrov', *Kommunist*, no. 1 (1976) pp. 55–65.

31. *SPR*, vyp. 15, p. 381.

32. *Vestnik statistiki*, no. 4 (1974) p. 91; *Narodnoe khozyaistvo SSSR v 1980g* (Moscow: Finansy i Statistika, 1981) p. 95; 'KPSS v tsifrakh', *Partiinaya zhizn'*, no. 14 (1973) p. 17, and no. 14 (1981) p. 17. See also Table 6.1.

33. V. Yagodkin, *Kommunist*, p. 62; V. Protopopov, 'Za effektivnost' nauchnykh kadrov', *Kommunist*, no. 6 (1978) p. 74.

34. See, for example, V. Polunin, 'Raikom i nauchnye kollektivy', *Kommunist*, no. 9 (1980) pp. 38–49.

35. V. Yagodkin, in *Kommunist*, p. 56, and V. Sergeev, 'Partiinaya organizatsiya nauchnogo uchrezhdeniya', *Kommunist*, no. 6 (1972) pp. 92–103; V. Protopopov, *Kommunist*, p. 78.

36. 'Partiinyi kontrol' v vuze', pp. 34–5.

37. A. Shumakov, 'Nauchnym issledovaniyam – vysokuyu effektivnost'', *Partiinaya zhizn'*, no. 2 (1974) p. 32; Yu. Burlin, 'Partorganizatsiya i effektivnost' vuzovskoi nauki', *Partiinaya zhizn'*, no. 20 (1976) p. 37.

38. *Filosofskii slovar'* (Moscow: Politizdat, 1972) pp. 268–9.

39. In addition to the decree criticising the party organisation of the Lebedev Physics Institute (in *SPR*, vyp. 11, pp. 275–9), see Yu. V. Sachkov and V. P. Chekurin, 'Filosofskie (metodologicheskie) seminary v nauchnykh uchrezhdeniyakh', *Vestnik Akademii nauk SSSR*, no. 4 (1980) p. 47; the decree issued by the Central Committee on 26 May 1981, 'O dal'neishem sovershenstvovanii partiinoi ucheby v svete reshenii XXVI s''ezda KPSS', *SPR*, vyp. 22, pp. 507–13, and Yu. A. Ovchinnikov, 'Zadachi filosofskikh (metodologicheskikh) seminarov', *Vestnik Akademii nauk SSSR*, no. 2 (1982) p. 53.

40. B. Chaplin, 'Raionnyi komitet partii', p. 47.

41. M. Zimyanin, 'Vysshaya shkola na novom etape', *Kommunist*, no. 3 (1980) p. 20.

42. For a recent example of the recognition of the conceptual independence of the natural sciences, see Yu. A. Ovchinnikov, 'Zadachi filosofskikh', p. 50.

43. See *Filosofskii slovar'*.
44. V. Yagodkin, 'Razrabotka problem i propaganda sotsialisticheskogo obraza zhizni – vazhneishaya zadacha v usloviyakh sovremmenoi ideologicheskoi bor'by', *Sotsiologicheskie issledovaniya*, no. 1 (1975) pp. 9–18; M. N. Rutkevich, 'Ideino-teoreticheskaya podgotovka nauchnykh kadrov', *Partiinaya zhizn'*, no. 10 (1976) pp. 24–9; A. F. Dobritsa, 'V avangarde ideiinogo vospitaniya studentchestva', *Vestnik vysshei shkoly*, no. 6 (1975) pp. 52–6; Yu. P. Sviridenko, 'Sovershenstvovat' partiinoe rukovodstvo kafedrami', *Vestnik vysshei shkoly*, no. 12 (1980) pp. 53–9.
45. Decree issued by the Central Committee on 26 April 1979, 'O dal'neishem uluchshenii ideologicheskoi, politiko–vospitatel'noi raboty', *SPR*, vyp. 20, pp. 319–31.
46. See Zhores Medvedev, *Soviet Science*, pp. 180–203; Arnost Kol'man, 'A Life in Soviet Science Reconsidered: The Adventure of Cybernetics in the Soviet Union', *Minerva*, vol. xvi, no. 3 (Autumn 1978) pp. 416–24, especially p. 418.
47. V. Yagodkin, *Kommunist*, p. 64.
48. Decrees issued by the Central Committee on 27 January 1977 and 15 January 1980, 'O deyatel'nosti sibirskogo otdeleniya Akademii nauk SSSR', *SPR*, vyp. 18, pp. 238–43, and 'O deyatel'nosti dal'nevo-stochnogo nauchnogo tsentra Akademii nauk SSSR po razvitiyu fundamental'nykh i prikladnykh issledovanii, povysheniyu effektivnosti i vnedreniyu nauchnykh dostizhenii v narodnoe khozyaistvo', *SPR*, vyp. 21, pp. 321–6.

8 CONCLUSION

1. Zhores A. Medvedev, *Soviet Science* (Oxford University Press, 1979) pp. 152–4.
2. Yu. A. Ovchinnikov, 'Zadachi filosofskikh (metodologicheskikh) seminarov', *Vestnik Akademii nauk SSSR*, no. 2 (1982) p. 50.
3. *XXII s''ezd KPSS: Stenograficheskii otchët* (Moscow: Politizdat, 1962) p. 344, and see the decree issued by the Central Committee on 23 November 1962, 'O razvitii ekonomiki SSSR i perestroike partiinogo rukovodstva narodnym khozyaistvom', *SPR*, vyp. 4, pp. 191–221.
4. See the decree issued by the Central Committee, 'Ob ob''edinenii promyshlennykh i sel'skikh oblastnykh, kraevykh partiinykh organizatsii', *Pravda* (17 November 1964) p. 1, and 'XXIII s''ezd KPSS: Otchëtnyi doklad TsK KPSS', *Pravda* (30 March 1966) p. 9.
5. For recent breakdowns of the party membership by occupation see 'KPSS v tsifrakh', *Partiinaya zhizn'*, no. 14 (1981) p. 19. For commentary on the changing character of the party membership see T. H. Rigby, 'Soviet Communist Party Membership Under Brezhnev', *Soviet Studies*, vol. xxviii, no. 3 (July 1976) pp. 317–37, and A. L. Unger, 'Soviet Communist Party Membership Under Brezhnev: A Comment', *Soviet Studies*, vol. xxix, no. 2 (April 1977) pp. 306–16.

6. See the decree issued by the Central Committee on 26 April 1979, 'O dal'neishem uluchshenii ideologicheskoi politiko-vospitatel'noi raboty', *SPR*, vyp. 20, pp. 319–31. See also *XXVI s"ezd KPSS: Stenograficheskii otchët*, vol. 1 (Moscow: Politizdat, 1981) pp. 94–8.

7. Jerry F. Hough, 'Soviet Succession: Issues and Personalities', *Problems of Communism* (September–October 1982) pp. 20–40, especially p. 32, and Sidney I. Ploss, 'Soviet Succession: Signs of Struggle', *Problems of Communism* (September–October 1982) pp. 41–52, especially pp. 46–7.

8. Moshe Lewin, *Political Undercurrents in Soviet Economic Debates*, (London: Pluto Press, 1975) pp. 279–280.

9. Ibid., pp. 264–77 and 294–9.

10. On the character of the rank and file membership of the party see T. H. Rigby, 'Soviet Communist Party Membership', and A. L. Unger, 'Soviet Communist Party Membership under Brezhnev'.

11. Roy A. Medvedev, *On Socialist Democracy* (London: Macmillan, 1975) pp. 120–1.

12. For example, the Leninskii *raikom* (district committee) of the Moscow City Party Organisation contains 66 scientific research and design institutes and higher educational institutions within its jurisdiction, employing more than 44 000 specialists and engineering-technical workers. See V. Protopopov, 'Za effektivnost' nauchnykh kadrov', *Kommunist*, no. 6 (1978) p. 71.

Bibliography

Abelson, Philip H., 'International Geophysics: Science Dominates Politics', *Science*, 190 (3 October 1975) p. 34.

Adams, Mark, 'Biology after Stalin: A Case Study', *Survey*, vol. 23, no. 1 (Winter 1977-8) pp. 53-80.

Alferov, M., 'Ideinaya zakalka nauchnykh kadrov', *Partiinaya zhizn'*, no. 15 (1972) pp. 54-60.

Amann, Ronald, 'The Chemical Industry: Its Level of Modernity and Technological Sophistication', in Ronald Amann, Julian Cooper and R. W. Davies (eds) with the assistance of Hugh Jenkins, *The Technological Level of Soviet Industry* (Newhaven and London: Yale University Press, 1977).

Avtorkhanov, A., *The Communist Party Apparatus* (Cleveland and New York: Meridian, 1966).

Azbel, Mark Ya., *Refusenik* (London: Hamish Hamilton, 1981).

Balashev, L. L., 'Voprosy nauchnoi informatsii v oblasti biologii', *Nauchno-tekhnicheskaya informatsiya*, seriya 2, no. 2 (1967) pp. 9-12.

Barinova, Z. B. *et al.*, 'Izucheniya nauchnykh zhurnalov kak kanalov svyazi', *Nauchno-tekhnicheskaya informatsiya*, seriya 2, no. 12 (1967) pp. 3-11.

Beilin, A. E., *Kadry spetsialistov SSSR* (Moscow and Leningrad: TsUNKhU Gosplana, 1935).

Belotserkovskii, O. M., 'Sovremennaya nauka i vuzy', *Vestnik Akademii nauk SSSR*, no. 7 (1975) pp. 36-42.

Belyaev, S., 'Rol' universiteta v podgotovke kadrov dlya nauk', *Vestnik Akademii nauk SSSR*, no. 3 (1976) pp. 31-5.

Blinov, N. and Sleptsov, N., 'Sotsiologicheskii portret studentov', *Molodoi kommunist* (September 1979) pp. 101-2.

Bol'shaya Sovetskaya Entsiklopediya, 2nd edn, 51 vols (Moscow: Bol'shaya Sovetskaya Entsiklopediya, 1949-58). Abbreviated *BSE*.

Bol'shaya Sovetskaya Entsiklopediya, 3rd edn, 30 vols (Moscow: Bol'shaya Sovetskaya Entsiklopediya, 1970-8). Abbreviated *BSE*.

Borisov, Yu. S., 'Izmenenie sotsial'nogo sostava uchashchikhsya vo vysshikh i srednykh spetsial'nykh zavedeniyakh 1917-1940gg', in M. P. Kim (ed.), *Kul'turnaya revolyutsiya v SSSR 1917-1965gg* (Moscow: Nauka, 1967).

Burbulya, Yu. T., and Korbarskaya, V. P., 'Issledovanie tsitiruemosti matematicheskoi literatury', *Nauchno-tekhnicheskaya informatsiya*, seriya 2, no. 2 (1978) pp. 10-14.

Burlin, Yu., 'Partorganizatsiya i effektivnost' vuzovskoi nauki', *Partiinaya zhizn'*, no. 20 (1976) pp. 32-8.

Butenko, R. G., 'Vashe kreslo v Akademii', *Sovetskaya Rossiya* (23 April 1980) p. 4.

Byrnes, Robert F., 'Soviet-American Academic Exchange', *Survey*, vol. 22, no. 3–4 (Summer–Autumn 1976) pp. 23–38.

Callen, Earl, 'US-Soviet Scientific Exchange in the Age of Detente', *Survey*, vol. 21, no. 4 (Autumn 1975) pp. 52–9.

Chaplin, B., 'Raionnyi komitet partii i nauchno-tekhnicheskaya intelligentsiya', *Kommunist*, no. 7 (1974) pp. 42–53.

'Chastichnye izmeneniya v ustave KPSS, vnesennye XXIV s''ezdom KPSS', *Partiinaya zhizn'*, no. 9 (1971) pp. 10–12.

Chernovolenko, V. F., Ossovskii, V. L. and Paniotto, V. I., *Prestizh professii i problemy sotsial'no-professional'noi orientatsii molodezhi* (Kiev: Naukova Dumka, 1979).

Chutkerashvili, E. V., *Kadry dlya nauki* (Moscow: Vysshaya shkola, 1968).

Crane, Diana, 'Transnational Networks in Basic Science', in Robert O. Keohane and Joseph S. Nye Jr (eds), *Transnational Relations and World Politics* (Cambridge, Mass.: Harvard University Press, 1972) pp. 235–51.

Davidson-Frame, J. and Carpenter, Mark P., 'International Research Collaboration', *Social Studies of Science*, vol. 9, no. 4 (November 1979) pp. 481–97.

Dobritsa, A. F., 'V avangarde ideiinogo vospitaniya studentchestva', *Vestnik vysshei shkoly*, no. 6 (1975) pp. 52–6.

Dobrov, G. M., Klimenyuk, V. N., Odrin, V. M. and Savel'ev, A. A., *Organizatsiya nauki* (Kiev: Naukova Dumka, 1970).

Dobrov, G. M., Klimenyuk, V. N., Smirnov, L. P. and Savel'ev, A. A., *Potensial nauki* (Kiev: Naukova Dumka, 1969).

Dubov, R. L., 'Podvedenie itogov sotsialisticheskogo sorevnovaniya v akademicheskikh institutakh', *Vestnik Akademii nauk SSSR*, no. 4 (1980) pp. 106–8.

Duzhenkov, V. I., 'Organizatsiya fundamental'nykh issledovanii v akademiyakh nauk soyuznykh respublik', in *Organizatsiya nauchnoi deyatel'nosti* (Moscow: Nauka, 1968).

Effektivnost' nauchnykh issledovanii (Alma-Ata: Nauka KSSR, 1978).

Elyutin, V. P., 'Za organicheskoe edinstvo nauchnoi i uchebnoi raboty', *Vestnik vysshei shkoly*, no. 9 (1972) pp. 3–7.

Elyutin, V. P. 'Vysshaya shkola v svete reshenii XXIV s''ezda KPSS', *Partiinaya zhizn'*, no. 7 (1973) pp. 8–16.

Esareva, S. F., *Osobennosti deyatel'nosti prepodavatelya vysshei shkoly* (Leningrad: izd. LGU, 1974).

Fainsod, Merle, *How Russia is Ruled* (Cambridge, Mass.: Harvard University Press, 1967).

Filosofkii slovar' (Moscow: Politizdat, 1972).

Fortescue, Stephen, 'Research Institute Party Organizations and the Right of Control', *Soviet Studies*, xxxv, no. 2 (April 1983) pp. 175–95.

Frolov, B. A., 'Motivatsiya tvorchestva v nauchnom kollektive', in *Sotsial'no psikhologicheskie problemy nauki* (Moscow: Nauka, 1973) pp. 135–65.

Gaston, J., 'Communication and the Reward System of Science: A Study of a National "Invisible College"', *Sociological Review Monograph*, 18, pp. 25–41.

Gervitz, L. Yu. and Rozanov, V. V., 'Analiz opyta, problem i perspektiv primeneniya programmno-tselevykh metodov v sisteme AN SSSR', *Vestnik Akademii nauk SSSR*, no. 1 (1981) pp. 77–81.

Golovanov, L. V., 'Sistema upravleniya naukoi v SSSR: voprosy ee sovershenstvovaniya', in *Nauchnoe upravlenie obshchestvom*, vyp. 3 (Moscow: Mysl', 1969).

Gottikh, B. P. and Dyumenton, G. G., 'Lichnye nauchnye kommunikatsii i organizatsiya fundamental'nykh issledovanii', *Vestnik Akademii nauk SSSR*, vol. 12 (1979) pp. 65–78.

Graham, Loren R., *Science and Philosophy in the Soviet Union* (London: Allen Lane, 1971).

Graham, Loren R., 'The Role of the Academy of Sciences', *Survey*, vol. 23, no. 1 (Winter 1977–8) pp. 117–33.

Granovskii, Yu. B., *Naukometricheskii analiz informatsionnykh potokov v khimii* (Moscow: Nauka, 1980).

Gustafson, Thane, 'Why Doesn't Soviet Science Do Better Than It Does?', in Linda L. Lubrano and Susan Gross Solomon (eds), *The Social Context of Soviet Science* (Folkestone: Wm Dawson, 1980).

Hagstrom, W. O., *The Scientific Community* (New York: Basic Books, 1965).

Harasymiw, B., '*Nomenklatura*: The Soviet Communist Party's Leadership Recruitment System', *Canadian Journal of Political Science*, vol. 2, no. 4 (December 1969) pp. 493–512.

Hill, Ronald J. and Frank, Peter, *The Soviet Communist Party* (London: George Allen & Unwin, 1981).

Hough, Jerry F., 'Soviet Succession: Issues and Personalities', *Problems of Communism* (September–October 1982) pp. 20–40.

Hough, Jerry F. and Fainsod, Merle, *How the Soviet Union is Governed* (Cambridge, Mass., and London: Harvard University Press, 1979).

Jevons, F. P., *The Teaching of Science* (London: Allen & Unwin, 1969).

Joravsky, David, *The Lysenko Affair* (Cambridge, Mass.: Harvard University Press, 1971).

Kaiser, R., *Russia: The People and the Power* (Harmondsworth: Penguin Books, 1977).

Kapitsa, P. L., *Zhizn' dlya nauki, Lomonosov, Franklin, Rezerford, Lanzheven* (Moscow: Znanie, 1965).

Kapitsa, P. L., *Teoriya, Eksperiment, Praktika* (Moscow: Znanie, 1966).

Kelle, V. Zh., Kugel', S. A. and Makeshin, N. I., 'Sotsiologicheskie aspekty organizatsii truda nauchnykh rabotnikov v sfere fundamental'nykh issledovanii (po materialam konkretno-sotsiologicheskogo issledovaniya)', in *Sotsiologicheskie problemy nauchnoi deyatel'nosti* (Moscow: Institut sotsiologicheskikh issledovanii AN SSSR, 1978).

Khranilov, P., 'Otraslevoi ili politekhnicheskii', *Izvestiya* (5 April 1972) p. 3.

Kirillin, V. A., 'Ob uchastii profsoyuzov v osushchestvlenii tekhnicheskogo progressa v narodnom khozyaistve', *Trud* (2 October 1968) p. 2.

Kirillin, V. A., *Vestnik Akademii nauk SSSR*, no. 5 (1976) pp. 47–50.

Kirillov-Ugryumov, V., 'Dve stupeni vuza', *Izvestiya* (21 May 1972) p. 3.

Kirillov-Ugryumov, V., 'Kadry nauki', *Pravda* (29 May 1975) p. 3.

Kirillov-Ugryumov, V., 'Sistema attestatsii nauchnykh kadrov', *Kommunist*, no. 1 (1976) pp. 55–65.

Kneen, P. H., *Higher Education and Cultural Revolution in the USSR*, Soviet Industrialisation Project, Unpublished Discussion Paper, no. 5 (CREES, University of Birmingham, 1976).

Kol'man, Arnost, 'A Life in Soviet Science Reconsidered: The Adventure of Cybernetics in the Soviet Union', *Minerva*, vol. xvi, no. 3 (Autumn 1978) pp. 416–24.

Kolobashkin, V. M. and Ivanov, V. I., 'Vuzovskaya nauka na styke raznykh oblastei znaniya', *Vestnik Akademii nauk SSSR*, no. 9 (1980) pp. 43–8.

Komkov, G. D., Karpenko, O. M., Levshin, B. V. and Semenov, L. K., *Akademiya nauk shtab sovetskoi nauki* (Moscow: Nauka, 1968).

Komkov, G. D., Levshin, B. V. and Semenov, L. K., *Akademiya nauk SSSR* (Moscow: Nauka, 1974).

Kozhemako, V., 'Potentsial prakticheski bezgranichen...', *Pravda* (2 December 1970) p. 2.

KPSS v rezolyutsiyakh i resheniyakh s''ezdov, konferentsii i plenumov TsK, 8th edn, tom 4 (Moscow: Politizdat, 1970).

'KPSS v tsifrakh', *Partiinaya zhizn'*, no. 1 (1962) pp. 44–54.

'KPSS v tsifrakh', *Partiinaya zhizn'*, no. 14 (1973) pp. 9–26.

'KPSS v tsifrakh', *Partiinaya zhizn'*, no. 21 (1977) pp. 20–43.

'KPSS v tsifrakh', *Partiinaya zhizn'*, no. 14 (1981) pp. 13–26.

Krutov, V., 'Atmosfera poiska', *Izvestiya* (11 January 1972) p. 5.

Kugel', S. A., 'Struktura i dinamika nauchnykh kadrov', in *Upravlenie, planirovanie i organizatsiya nauchnykh i tekhnicheskikh issledovanii*, tom 2 (Moscow: VINITI, 1971).

Kugel', S. A. and Nikandrov, O. M., *Molodye inzhenery* (Moscow: Mysl', 1971).

Kugel', S. A., and Shelishch, P. B., 'Nauchnaya intelligentsiya SSSR: faktory i tendentsii razvitiya', *Sotsiologicheskie issledovaniya*, no. 1 (1979) pp. 33–42.

Kuhn, T. S., 'The Function of Measurement in Modern Physical Science', in H. Woolf (ed.), *Quantification* (New York: Bobbs-Merrill, 1961).

Kuhn, T. S., 'Scientific Paradigms', in B. Barnes (ed.), *The Sociology of Science* (Harmondsworth: Penguin Books, 1972).

Kuhn, T. S., *The Structure of Scientific Revolutions* (University of Chicago Press, 1972).

Kul'turnoe stroitel'stvo SSSR (Moscow: Gosstatizdat, 1956).

Kushnarev, G. P., 'Razrabotka metodiki konkretno-sotsiologicheskogo issledovaniya nauchnoi deyatel'nosti', in *Sotsiologicheskie problemy nauchnoi deyatel'nosti* (Moscow: Institut sotsiologicheskikh issledovanii AN SSSR, 1978).

Lane, David and O'Dell, Felicity, *The Soviet Industrial Worker* (Oxford: Martin Robertson, 1978).

Lange, K. A., *Organizatsiya upravleniya nauchnymi issledovaniyami* (Leningrad: Nauka, 1971).

Lebin, B. D. and Perfil'ev, M. N., *Kadry apparata upravleniya v SSSR* (Leningrad: Nauka, 1971).

Lebin, B. D. and Tsypkin, G. A., *Prava rabotnika nauki* (Leningrad: Nauka, 1971).

Leiman, I. I., *Nauka kak sotsial'nyi institut* (Leningrad: Nauka, 1971).

Lewin, Moshe, *Political Undercurrents in Soviet Economic Debates* (London: Pluto Press, 1975).

Löwenhardt, John, 'Scientist-entrepreneurs in the Soviet Union', *Survey*, vol. 20, no. 4 (Autumn 1974) pp. 113–21.

Lubrano, Linda L., 'Scientific Collectives: Behaviour of Soviet Scientists in

Basic Research', in Linda L. Lubrano and Susan Gross Solomon (eds), *The Social Context of Soviet Science* (Folkestone: Wm. Dawson, 1980) pp. 101–36.

Lubrano, Linda L. and Berg, John K., 'Scientists in the USA and USSR', *Survey*, vol. 23, no. 1 (Winter 1977–8) pp. 161–93.

Matthews, Mervyn, 'Soviet Students – Some Sociological Perspectives', *Soviet Studies*, vol. xxvi, no. 1 (1975) pp. 86–108.

Matthews, Mervyn, *Privilege in the Soviet Union* (London: Allen & Unwin, 1978).

Medvedev, Roy A., *On Socialist Democracy* (London: Macmillan, 1975).

Medvedev, Zhores A., *The Rise and Fall of T. D. Lysenko* (New York: Columbia University Press, 1969).

Medvedev, Zhores A., *The Medvedev Papers* (London: Macmillan, 1971).

Medvedev, Zhores A., 'Two Decades of Dissidence', *New Scientist*, vol. 72 (1976) pp. 264–7.

Medvedev, Zhores A., *Soviet Science* (Oxford and Melbourne: Oxford University Press, 1979).

Meissner, Boris, 'The 26th Congress and Soviet Domestic Politics', *Problems of Communism* (May–June 1981) pp. 1–23.

Merton, Robert K., 'Priorities in Scientific Discovery', *American Sociological Review*, xxii (1957) pp. 635–59.

Merton, Robert K., 'Singletons and Multiples in Scientific Discovery', *Proceedings of the American Philosophical Society*, CV5 (October 1961) pp. 470–86.

Moskovskaya gorodskaya i moskovskaya oblastnaya organizatsii KPSS v tsifrakh (Moscow: Moskovskii rabochii, 1972).

Moskva v tsifrakh (1966–1970 gg) (Moscow: Statistika, 1972).

Moskva v tsifrakh (Moscow: Finansy i Statistika, 1981).

Mulkay, M. J., *The Social Process of Innovation* (London and Basingstoke: Macmillan, 1972).

Mullins, Nicholas C., 'The Development of a Scientific Speciality: The Phage Group and the Origins of Molecular Biology', *Minerva*, vol. 10, no. 1 (1972) pp. 51–82.

Nalimov, V. V. and Mul'chenko, Z. M., *Naukometriya* (Moscow: Nauka, 1969).

Narin, Francis and Carpenter, Mark P., 'National Publication and Citation Comparisons', *Journal of the American Society for Information Science*, vol. 26 (March–April 1975) pp. 80–93.

Narodnoe khozyaistvo SSSR (Moscow: Sotsekgiz, 1932).

Narodnoe khozyaistvo SSSR v 1956g (Moscow: Gosstatizdat, 1957).

Narodnoe khozyaistvo SSSR v 1960g (Moscow: Gosstatizdat, 1961).

Narodnoe khozyaistvo SSSR v 1961g (Moscow: Gosstatizdat, 1962).

Narodnoe khozyaistvo SSSR v 1962g (Moscow: Gosstatizdat, 1963).

Narodnoe khozyaistvo SSSR v 1963g (Moscow: Gosstatizdat, 1964).

Narodnoe khozyaistvo SSSR v 1970g (Moscow: Statistika, 1971).

Narodnoe khozyaistvo SSSR v 1973g (Moscow: Statistika, 1974).

Narodnoe khozyaistvo SSSR v 1979g (Moscow: Statistika, 1980).

Narodnoe khozyaistvo SSSR v 1980g (Moscow: Finansy i Statistika, 1981).

Narodnoe obrazovanie, nauka i kul'tura v SSSR (Moscow: Statistika, 1971).

Narodnoe obrazovanie, nauka i kul'tura v SSSR (Moscow: Statistika, 1977).
Nauchnye kadry Leningrada (Leningrad: Nauka, 1973).
Nauchno-tekhnicheskaya revolyutsiya i izmenenie struktury nauchnykh kadrov SSSR (Moscow: Nauka, 1973).
'Neprimirimost' k burzhuaznoi ideologii', *Pravda* (23 November 1970) p. 1.
Nesmeyanov, A. N., 'Nauka i proizvodstvo', *Kommunist*, no. 2 (1956) pp. 33–48.
Nye, J. D., 'Russians at Conferences' (correspondence), *Nature*, vol. 249 (3 May 1974) p. 8.
'O rabote partiinoi organizatsii Instituta ekonomiki Akademii nauk SSSR po vypolneniyu postanovleniya TsK KPSS, O merakh po dal'neishemu razvitiyu obshchestvennykh nauk i povysheniya ikh roli v kommunisticheskom stroitel'stve', *Kommunist*, no. 1 (1972) pp. 3–5.
'Ob ob''edinenii promyshlennykh i sel'skikh oblastnykh, kraevykh partiinykh organizatsii', *Pravda* (17 November 1964) p. 1.
Organizatsionno-pravovye voprosy rukovodstva naukoi v SSSR (Moscow: Nauka, 1973).
Osnovnye printsipy i obshchie problemy upravleniya naukoi (Moscow: Nauka, 1973).
Ovchinnikov, Yu. A., 'Zadachi filosofskikh (metodologicheskikh) seminarov', *Vestnik Akademii nauk SSSR*, no. 2 (1982) pp. 48–56.
'Partiinyi kontrol' v vuze', *Partiinaya zhizn'*, no. 6 (1973) pp. 31–7.
Ploss, Sidney I., 'Soviet Succession: Signs of Struggle', *Problems of Communism* (September–October 1982) pp. 41–52.
Podgotovka kadrov v SSSR 1927–1931gg (Moscow-Leningrad: Sotsekgiz, 1933).
Polunin, V., 'Raikom i nauchnye kollektivy', *Kommunist*, no. 9 (1980) pp. 38–49.
Popovsky, Mark, 'Science in Blinkers', *Index on Censorship*, vol. 9, no. 4 (August 1980) pp. 14–18.
Popovsky, Mark, *Science in Chains* (London: Collins & Harvill, 1980).
Poshataev, V. V., 'Nauchnyi kollektiv kak sfera formirovaniya individual'nosti', in *Nauchnoe upravlenie obshchestvom*, vyp 5 (Moscow: Mysl', 1971).
Pravdin, A., 'Inside the CPSU Central Committee' (interview with Mervyn Matthews), *Survey*, vol. 20, no. 4 (Autumn 1974) pp. 94–104.
Price, Derek de Solla, *Little Science, Big Science* (New York: Columbia University Press, 1963).
Price, Derek de Solla, 'Science and Technology: Distinctions and Interrelationships', in B. Barnes (ed.), *The Sociology of Science* (Harmondsworth: Penguin Books, 1972).
Price, Derek de Solla and Beaver, Donald de B., 'Collaboration in an Invisible College', *American Psychologist*, vol. 21 (1966) pp. 1011–18.
Prokrovskii, V., 'Upravlenie effektivnost'yu nauki i tekhniki', *Ekonomicheskaya gazeta*, no. 32 (August 1977) p. 10.
Protopopov, V., 'Za effektivnost' nauchnykh kadrov', *Kommunist*, no. 6 (1978) pp. 71–82.
Rabkin, Ya. M., 'The Study of Science', *Survey*, vol. 23, no. 1 (Winter 1977–8) pp. 134–45.

Rassudovskii, V. A., *Gosudarstvennaya organizatsiya nauki v SSSR* (Moscow: Yuridicheskaya Literatura, 1971).

Rigby, T. H., *Communist Party Membership in the USSR 1917–67* (Princeton University Press, 1968).

Rigby, T. H., 'Soviet Communist Party Membership Under Brezhnev', *Soviet Studies*, vol. xxviii, no. 3 (July 1976) pp. 317–37.

Rubin, B. and Kolesnikov, Yu., *Student glazami sotsiologa* (izd. Rostovskogo Universiteta, 1968).

Rules of the CPSU (Moscow: Progress Publishers, 1977).

Rutkevich, M. N., 'Ideino-teoreticheskaya podgotovka nauchnykh kadrov', *Partiinaya zhizn'*, no. 10 (1976) pp. 24–9.

Rutkevich, M. N., 'Sovetskaya intelligentsiya: struktura i tendentsii razvitiya na sovremennom etape', *Sotsiologicheskie issledovaniya*, no. 2 (1980) pp. 63–74.

Rutkevich, M. N. and Filippov, F. R., *Sotsial'nye peremeshcheniya* (Moscow: Mysl', 1970).

Rutkevich, M. N. and Filippov, F. R., *Vysshaya shkola kak faktor izmeneniya sotsial'noi struktury sotsialisticheskogo obshchestva* (Moscow: Nauka, 1978).

Rzhanov, A. V., 'O nekotorykh putyakh povysheniya effektivnosti fundamental'nykh nauchnykh issledovanii', *Vestnik Akademii nauk SSSR*, no. 2 (1982) pp. 41–7.

Sachkov, Yu. V. and Chekurin, V. P., 'Filosofskie (metodologicheskie) seminary v nauchnykh uchrezhdeniyakh', *Vestnik Akademii nauk SSSR*, no. 4 (1980) pp. 42–53.

Sakharov, A. D., *Progress, Coexistence and Intellectual Freedom* (Harmondsworth: Penguin Books, 1969).

Sakharov, A. D., *Sakharov Speaks* (London: Collins & Harvill, 1974).

Schapiro L., *The Communist Party of the Soviet Union* (London: Methuen, 1970).

Schapiro, L., 'The General Department of the CC of the CPSU', *Survey*, vol. 21, no. 3 (Summer 1975) pp. 53–65.

Semenov, V., 'Fond dlya nauki', *Pravda* (27 December 1968) p. 2.

Serebrovskaya, K. B., 'Sovremennyi neformal'nyi kollektiv v fundamental'nykh issledovaniyakh', in *Sotsial'no-psikhologicheskie problemy nauki* (Moscow: Nauka, 1973) pp. 96–127.

Sergeev, V., 'Partiinaya organizatsiya nauchnogo uchrezhdeniya', *Kommunist*, no. 6 (1972) pp. 92–103.

Sergeeva, I. V., 'Kollektiv i lichnost' v nauke', *Sotsial'nye issledovaniya*, vyp. 3 (Moscow: Nauka, 1970) pp. 178–88.

Sheinin, Yu., *Science Policy: Problems and Trends* (Moscow: Progress Publishers, 1978).

Shelton, William R., 'Science in Siberia', *Bulletin of the Atomic Scientists* (February 1971) pp. 23–8.

Shmidt, O. Yu., 'Problema nauchnykh kadrov', *Vestnik Kommunisticheskoi Akademii*, kniga 37–8 (1930) pp. 15–23.

Shumakov, A., 'Nauchnym issledovaniyam – vysokuyu effektivnost'', *Partiinaya zhizn'*, no. 2 (1974) pp. 29–33.

Smith, Hedrick, *The Russians* (London: Times Books, 1976).

Sotsial'no-professional'naya orientatsiya molodezhi (Tartu: Tartuskii Gosudarstvennyi Universitet, 1973).

Spravochnik partiinogo rabotnika, vols. 1–22 (Moscow: Politizdat, 1957–82 and continuing). Abbreviated *SPR*.

Stepanyan, Ts. A. *et al.* (eds), *Klassy, sotsial'nye sloi i gruppy v SSSR* (Moscow: Nauka, 1968).

Strana Sovetov za 50 let: sbornik statisticheskikh materialov (Moscow: Statistika, 1967).

Suslov, M. A., in *Vestnik Akademii nauk SSSR*, no. 1 (1976) pp. 4–6.

Sviridenko, Yu. P., 'Sovershenstvovat' partiinoe rukovodstvo kafedrami', *Vestnik vysshei shkoly*, no. 12 (1980) pp. 53–9.

Tal'roze, V. L. and Tsyganov, S. A., 'Vozmozhnosti ispol'zovaniya programmno-tselevykh metodov pri planirovanii fundamental'nykh issledovanii na urovne nauchnogo uchrezhdeniya', *Vestnik Akademii nauk SSSR*, no. 1 (1981) pp. 57–61.

Tatu, M., *Power in the Kremlin* (London: Collins, 1969).

Turchin, Valentin, *The Inertia of Fear* (Oxford: Martin Robertson, 1981).

Unger, A. L., 'Soviet Communist Party Membership Under Brezhnev: A Comment', *Soviet Studies*, vol. XXIX, no. 2 (April 1977) pp. 306–16.

Upravlenie, planirovanie i organizatsiya nauchnykh i tekhnicheskikh issledovanii, tom 3 (Moscow: VINITI, 1970).

Ustavy Akademii nauk SSSR, 1724–1974gg (Moscow: Nauka, 1974).

Velikhov, Ye. and Prokhorov, A., 'Kak gotovit' issledovatelei', *Izvestiya* (25 January 1977) p. 2.

Vestnik statistiki, no. 4 (1962) p. 64.

Vestnik statistiki, no. 4 (1974) pp. 85–95.

Vestnik statistiki, no. 8 (1981) p. 78.

Vladimirov, N. and Afanas'ev, I., 'Uchenye i lzheuchenye', *Literaturnaya gazeta* (5 June 1974) p. 11, and continued (11 June 1974) p. 12.

Volkenstein, M., 'Perekrëstki otkrytii', *Izvestiya* (9 May 1972) p. 5.

Vucinich, A., *The Soviet Academy of Sciences* (Stanford University Press, 1956).

De Witt, Nicholas, *Education and Professional Employment in the USSR* (Washington, D. C.: NSF, 1961).

XVIII s"ezd VKP (b): Stenograficheskii otchët (Moscow: Politizdat, 1939).

XXII s"ezd KPSS: Stenograficheskii otchët, 2 vols (Moscow: Politizdat, 1962).

'XXIII s"ezd KPSS: Otchëtnyi doklad TsK KPSS', *Pravda* (30 March 1966) p. 9.

XXIV s"ezd KPSS: Stenograficheskii otchët, 2 vols (Moscow: Politizdat, 1971).

XXVI s"ezd KPSS: Stenograficheskii otchët, 3 vols (Moscow: Politizdat, 1981).

Yagodkin, V., 'Partiinaya zhizn' v nauchnykh kollektivakh', *Kommunist*, no. 11 (1972) pp. 51–64.

Yagodkin, V., 'Partiinye organizatsii vuzov i vospitanie molodykh spetsialistov', *Partiinaya zhizn'*, no. 18 (1973) pp. 57–64.

Yagodkin, V., 'Razrabotka problem i propaganda sotsialisticheskogo obraza zhizni – vazhneishaya zadacha v usloviyakh sovremennoi ideologicheskoi bor'by', *Sotsiologicheskie issledovaniya*, no. 1 (1975) pp. 9–18.

Yamolovich, O., 'Ideinaya zakalka nauchno-tekhnicheskoi intelligentsii', *Partiinaya zhizn*, no. 16 (1970) pp. 53–9.

Yanovskii, R., 'Ideinost' uchenogo', *Sovetskaya Rossiya* (28 August 1970) p. 2.

Yanovskii, R., *Politicheskaya ucheba v nauchnom kollektive* (Moscow: Politizdat, 1974).

Yanowitch, Murray, *Social and Economic Inequality in the Soviet Union* (London: Martin Robertson, 1977).

Yanowitch, Murray and Dodge, Norton, 'The Social Evaluation of Occupations in the Soviet Union', *Slavic Review*, vol. 28, no. 1 (March 1969) pp. 619–44.

Zaleski, E., Kozlowski, J.P., Weinert, H., Davies, R. W., Berry, M. J. and Amann R., *Science Policy in the USSR* (Paris: OECD, 1969).

Ziman, John, 'Soviet Science and the Invisible College', *The Listener* (10 June 1976) pp. 725–6.

Zimyanin, M., 'Vysshaya shkola na novom etape', *Kommunist*, no. 3 (1980) pp. 15–27.

Index

135

Index